God's Breaking Heart

Chris M. Hibbard

God's Breaking Heart

And Other Short Stories
Terreldor Press Shorts

TP

Terreldor Press
Houston, TX
http://www.Terreldor.com
publishing@Terreldor.com
ISBN 10: 0615986110 (tpo.)
ISBN 978-0615986111
Published by Terreldor Press

To receive release notifications for new books by Chris M. Hibbard, email publishing@Terreldor.com with "Adventures in Terreldor" in Subject line.

Printed in the United States of America
First Edition

Terreldor Press   http://Terreldor.com

Contents

Preface

You are holding a collection of short fiction from Terreldor Press: a novella titled God's Breaking Heart, which comprises the bulk of this collection, and three additional short stories.

The works in this collection have encouraged over a half-million readers, and garnered thousands of positive reviews on the major online ebook retailers. This is the first time any of them has been available in print. The reader should be aware, the three short stories which follow God's Breaking Heart have at some point or another been available without charge on many popular ebook sites. You may have obtained these additional short stories for free. We hope you will enjoy having them in printed form, bound with the title novella.

ஜ *Terreldor Press* ஜ

God's Breaking Heart

When God is generous to show us, and we are wise enough to observe, we catch glimpses of the anguish He feels at seeing His children hurt themselves, and hurt each other. When we spread our pain to others, or multiply it through unforgiveness, I believe it breaks God's heart. The path of forgiveness is characterized by that first step, which is monumentally more difficult than the rest of the journey. Consider, God may have more *agents* than angels. His agents are everywhere, acting on His behalf, and anyone can become one of them. It is truly a gift to realize: the way you choose to react to others is a choice between being an *agent* or an *instigator*, and what you pass on to others may spread further than you could ever imagine.

Robert at Risk

Since the accident, Robert Stevens found he could no longer concentrate at work, and recently lost his job. Without insurance, he could no longer afford the counselor he'd been seeing, and he'd fallen deeper into depression. Robert had become a desperate man.

It's all his fault, he thought to himself, on the way home from the bank. Behind on his mortgage, he was nearly complete in the process of refinancing his home. The loan officer tried to validate his employment a second time, and learned Robert had none—and so his loan was denied. However, Robert wasn't blaming the man at the bank. His mind was fixed on the object of his long-held hatred.

Mentally, he unshelved an old plan—a hateful, harmful plan he'd once resolved to abandon. He glanced at his watch and noted the date once again, steeling his resolve.

I've thought about this long enough. What do I have to lose?

He would head to the convenience store he'd been visiting for the past months, but first, a quick stop home. He drove through a red light on the way, causing several cars to skid on the wet pavement to avoid hitting him. One car stuck another, damaging both headlights on the one, and the tail lights of the other. Glass and plastic lay strewn in the middle of the intersection. He angrily waved off the cars honking at him.

Tom's Despair

Most days weren't easy for Tom. Today was rainy, which was better than snow or heavy rain, but worse than hot and sunny. If he didn't dry out by the time the sun went down, he was going to need something to use as a blanket. He thought about going early to the underpass where he slept, but thought better of it. If he got some more change, he could buy whiskey instead of wine. He wasn't proud this was the type of reasoning that governed his day, but then, he wasn't proud of much.

He thought for just a second of that extra stash he kept, but pushed it to the back of his mind. It was his last discipline, keeping it for a true emergency, like breaking a leg, or imminent death.

This was a good corner. Nothing really bad ever happened to Tom at this corner, but then, nothing really good did either. Once someone gave him a five dollar bill, but come to think of it, that was on the next street down.

He watched the cars drive by, and stop when the light tuned red. When the cars stopped at the intersection, it was his best change for some cash. Most walkers wouldn't acknowledge him. It was a social contract; if they didn't acknowledge him, he couldn't acknowledge them. If he broke this contract, he'd instigate complaints, and the next day, some flat-foot would run him off. But cars—when they stopped for a red light—if he could catch their drivers' eyes, most times they would *have to* acknowledge him, and *then*, a rolled down window and a few coins, or even a dollar or two might come his way. They weren't so afraid to see him from inside their cars. They could always drive away if he made a ruckus.

He saw a small, thin man walk by, who nearly stepped out into the street to avoid him. He was wearing a fancy suit, and a nice overcoat. He walked as if he were in a race. Tom saw his eyes, before they darted away. He looked happy, but also worried, or perhaps angry. It was a hard expression to read.

Tom was hurting. He had a cold in his chest, but if he coughed much at all, no one would see him, or worse, see him *too much*, and he'd get run off his corner again. So he let out muffled coughs when he had to, and held his breath when a passerby looked like they might stop. He couldn't wait for the day to end, and that blessed trip to the cheapest liquor store within walking distance. Then, back to a nice box under the overpass, and maybe a blanket.

Timothy's Choice

Timothy walked from the bank, on his way to an early lunch. He nearly bounced along the sidewalk on the way to his favorite restaurant. He was a short, thin man, with a quick gait that carried him swiftly on his way.

Serves him right, he thought of Robert Stevens, *trying to hide his employment status. He knew the terms of the refinance.* He held no remorse for Robert, even though he would likely lose his home—a house that was mostly paid-off. *Besides,* he thought again, *I saw his bloodshot eyes and flushed complexion—the man's obviously a drunk. It's no wonder he lost his job.*

He wondered if he should feel guilty, instead of this

strange sense of accomplishment after checking the man's employment status a second time, just before signing off on the loan. He shrugged his shoulders nonchalantly and continued on his way.

After lunch, he wondered if he should've had the second martini he'd ordered to reward himself for his extra thoroughness. His hypocrisy shamed him for a moment: the thought came to his mind in the form of something his daughter had said to him in an argument.

"You're no better yourself," she'd yelled, and though the context was different, it was all hypocrisy. It was the last time he'd spoken to her, years ago.

A good banker is prudent—not a prude, he told himself, whisking away all concern and banishing all thoughts of his daughter from his mind. It started raining again, and he pulled open his umbrella. He passed the homeless man he'd seen earlier, standing at the corner, holding a coffee cup in his hand, begging for change.

"What's this city coming to?" he mumbled under his breath. "He should be arrested."

With his mind considering how early he could possibly leave work that evening, he missed the blinking word, *STOP*, on the crosswalk. Just after he stepped into the street, he sensed the homeless man rush toward him, and he spun around in fear. He expected an attack or mugging—anything but this ragged man grabbing his overcoat with both hands and yanking him backward hard enough to topple the two of them onto the sidewalk. He rolled off the homeless man and sprang to his feet, not sure whether he should run, or somehow try to defend himself. The man smelled of urine and vomit, and Timothy tried in vain to brush the man's scent from his overcoat.

A women near him on the sidewalk grabbed Timothy's arm, turning him to face her.

"You stepped right in front of that bus," she yelled. He spun once again, and watched the back of the bus speed quickly away from him. "He saved your life, this man," she said, waving her hand at the homeless man, still lying on the ground.

"Oh," Timothy responded in shock, his mind empty of any useful response. He offered his hand to help the man up, then pulled his hand away when he remembered the state of the man's soiled clothing.

The homeless man grasped at Timothy's hand and began to stand, then toppled back onto the ground, striking his head again on the concrete step of the shop behind him when Timothy withdrew it.

The man propped himself up and sat on the wet step, holding his head in his hands. He let out a little moan as he rubbed the back of his head.

Oh great, Timothy thought, *now he'll sue me.* His eyes rolled just before he caught the disapproving glare from the woman who'd grabbed his arm.

"Look," he said to the seated man, "I'm sorry you hit your head. You should...probably see a doctor. At least get some aspirin." Reaching into his pocket, he fished out some change and dropped it near the man's overturned cup. A few of the coins he dropped rolled into the street. He saw the crosswalk sign shine a steady, *WALK*, and so he did, right across the street, and away from the man sitting on the wet sidewalk, and the small crowd staring his way.

Turning back, he saw the woman who'd stopped him, staring at him with a shocked, indignant expression. She couldn't see it, but Timothy was distraught with awkward embarrassment. His curt response was how he'd learned to deal with anxiety; it was his way of hiding it from others.

Back in his office, Timothy was badly shaken. He realized how unlikely it was the homeless man should have so violently, so selflessly reached out to save him. He was no fool; he knew how poorly he'd treated the man who in all likelihood saved his life. His face grew red and his heart raced.

I should go back, I should thank him. At the very least, I should make sure he didn't badly hurt himself. He knew many things he should do, but he found the embarrassment of these choices, the humiliation he might feel, as insurmountable. Since he walked away from his family, years ago, Timothy had learned to shun nearly all human interaction. To have a stranger touch him, nevertheless topple him right on top of himself, was as distasteful to him as he could imagine.

He pushed the thoughts from his mind, and tried to focus on work.

Timothy checked his computer for his next meeting, and was relieved to see it wasn't for another hour. He recalled it was another loan he'd planned to deny. It was perhaps the strangest visit over a loan application he'd seen. His mind slipped back to his memories of his encounter with the woman, when he met her the previous week.

◆•◆• •◆•◆

A middle-aged woman in disheveled clothes arrived at his office running slightly late, seeking a loan for a homeless shelter. It was another refinance, in the name of a local ministry who had fallen on hard times in the recent economic downturn. The donations they depended on had fallen, and they couldn't keep up with their mortgage payments.

The ministry had a soup kitchen, and a large room of cots for emergency weather, open to any homeless person seeking shelter from freezing temperatures or rainstorms. Timothy recalled a sense of confusion over the meeting. The woman—what was her name? *Mary,* he called up from his computer. Mary looked like she dressed from the bargain rack. He saw her roots needed dyeing, and her nails were a mess. She'd carried a monstrous purse he was sure was a knock-off of an expensive brand. Timothy found it ironic this woman was meeting with him concerning a very large loan. *Why,* he'd thought, *this bag-lady looks like she couldn't have filled out the application.*

After his first meeting with her, he told her he would need to spend some time looking over her application, validating certain aspects of it, and sent her out of his office.

He'd planned to ignore it, not even go through the motions, and simply reject the organization's refinance. After he sent her out, he waited fifteen minutes before leaving work for the day, though it was only mid-afternoon. Disappointed, he saw her in the office foyer, just ending an inappropriately loud call on her cell phone. She walked to the parking garage just ahead of him. Timothy hung back enough not to risk a conversation with her. He saw her climb into a disheveled old car he would've guessed was abandoned.

How can this bag-lady be in charge of such a large loan application? he wondered. When he looked into it the following day, he found she was on the board of directors of a large ministry, and yet, was an unpaid volunteer. Her personal financials were horrid, but she wasn't guaranteeing the loan; the ministry was. The building they wanted to refinance was on prime downtown real estate.

"What kind of board would trust their application to her?" he'd scoffed under his breath.

Tom's Spare Change of Fate

With his head throbbing, Tom cursed himself for helping the man—he should've let him get hit by the bus.

As soon as he thought it, he rejected the notion. *What then,* he asked himself, *get hit by his body, after the bus hit him?*

"Tom," he mumbled to himself, "you couldn't live with yourself if you let the man die."

"That's an odd choice of words," he answered himself aloud. "I can't live with myself as it is."

He cradled his head in his hands, propping his elbows on his knees. His head throbbed viciously. He held his breath and reached back to feel the back of his head where it struck the concrete step. He expected it to be wet, but now it was also warm. He checked his hand; even in the failing light, he could see there was blood on it.

What now, Tom? he asked himself silently. He knew a

headache like this wouldn't get better with booze. *My one way out of pain...stolen from me.*

For a short moment, he felt rage for the man he blamed for his headache, but it brought a surge of adrenalin, and the throbbing in his head nearly overtook him. He swooned, falling onto his side—more pain. Passersby stared at him, he saw from the corner of his eye, and he knew it wasn't a *money-giving* kind of stare, it was a *complain-to-the-police* kind of stare.

If he breathed shallowly and closed his eyes, the throbbing subsided enough to think for a moment.

It's not getting any better from here, Tom, a voice in his head mocked him. *This is your ticket out.* He let out a muffled sob; he found he believed it. Just to be sure, he waited an hour. The throbbing pain in his head only got worse. He held his breath once again, and pulled something from his pocket. It was a thin sheet of plastic, folded again and again, then taped shut. He clutched it in his palm, holding it up to his gaze. He tore through the tape, unfolding the plastic to reveal a one hundred dollar bill. It was the most money he'd held since he found himself living on the streets. *And I've held onto it,* he cursed himself again, *for five whole years.*

Long enough, Tom. Long enough for this life of pain. The voice in his head sounded odd, and cruel. *You won't get this chance again.* He knew it was true. He'd broken his most sacred promise; he'd opened his makeshift wallet and taken the money out. He knew, for better or worse, he wouldn't have the money at sunrise.

With something to focus on, he could withstand the pain a little. He so desperately needed something to look forward to, even a plan to end his own life.

"It will feel wonderful," he mumbled aloud, "better than whiskey—and in the morning, no craving, no pain—ever; no pain ever again."

He needed a moment to rest, to let his pulse slow, so he could stand the throbbing pain he knew would come when he stood. He thought through the plan in his head, and it brought him a sick kind of calm. He knew where to find a heroin dealer not far away. A hundred dollars would buy enough heroin to do the job. He had only a mile or so to walk.

That's not what the money is for, a fleeting thought cautioned him. *It's to find Alex. He deserves to know what happened to you.* When he tried to consider this, the pain became nearly unbearable.

No one cares about you. Your son only wants to put you in rehab. The people who pass you by won't even look at you; not even the man you saved from the bus cares! You have only pain left in this life, and no one cares.

It was a door closed off to him; more pain was not an option. He stuffed the money deep into his pocket, and rested to gather his strength enough to stand. *It won't be long now, Tom,* he thought, *not long now.*

Sam's Cares

Sam was driving to an appliance repair store, to pick up a part for his broken kitchen stove. He was motivated by the prospect of spending another weekend eating food prepared in the microwave.

He rarely drove so far downtown, and he badly wanted to get home before rush hour.

When he reached the city, Sam drove his car with care; he didn't like driving downtown. Any traffic rules that changed according to the day of the week, or worse, according to the time of day, were unreasonable in his mind.

He came to a stop at a traffic light and craned his neck in search of any strange traffic signs. When he looked to his left, he saw a man in soiled clothes with a scruffy beard sitting on the concrete step of the store at the corner, trying to stand. His head had been in his hands, as if he were distraught, or injured.

Sam rolled his window down, and called to the man.

"Hey buddy, are you all right? Do you need help?"

Nervously, the man on the curb fumbled with both hands to find his coffee cup. He held it out when he found it.

"Got any spare change, for a guy down on his luck?" he asked, wincing.

"Down on your luck, eh?" Sam smiled warmly as he spoke, and made direct eye contact with him. "Look," Sam went on, "I don't have any money I can give you, but how about a snack?" Sam leaned back and reached behind his seat. He grabbed one of the brown paper sacks he kept there, and tossed it to the beggar on the curb. "There's some water in there, and a few items you might find useful."

"Thank you, thank you sir! God bless you!" called Tom. It was a reaction of instinct—he'd practiced it long enough.

"Now what's wrong with your head?" Sam asked, rushing a bit as he noticed the cars on the cross-street just stopped as their traffic light turned red.

"Just a headache, that's..." The man's voice was drowned out by the sound of car horns. The traffic light Sam was waiting for had turned green, and the car ahead of him had crossed the intersection.

"Oh, I have something for that, friend. Let me see here." Sam dug wildly through his glove compartment. He was well aware of the cars blaring their horns at him. *"God, help me find it,"* he prayed silently. "Here it is!" he yelled, as if it would buy time from the angry drivers behind him.

Sam didn't take time to open the bottle of pain reliever; he simply tossed the bottle to Tom.

"Bless you, kind sir, you're an angel," the street man called after him. In the midst of the chaos around him, Sam saw something change in the man's eyes as he caught the bottle of medicine. Sam found *hope* in the man's eyes. Time seemed to crawl slowly by for Sam, as he felt a courage he rarely knew.

"Sir," Sam replied boldly to the aged stranger, with a conviction that shocked both men. "I am only a servant," he went on, "but the One I serve wants to lavishly bless you. He *cares* for you, more than you can know. Pray that you may find Him."

Sam carefully pressed the accelerator, and sped through the intersection. The drivers behind him, spent of their aggression, became consumed with the task of negotiating their vehicles through the intersection before the light turned once again red.

Tom's Hope

Tom was in a state of confusion. Dim hope glimmered in his mind. His thoughts warred with each other, both condemning him and encouraging him to *hope*. That man, a stranger, was willing to get a traffic ticket for him, and to give him food and medicine. Numbly, he opened the brown paper sack to find a treasure trove of items he was in immediate need of.

Why can't it be so? he finally demanded of himself. *Someone can care about me. Maybe my son, maybe one last time.*

In the bag, he found a sealed bottle of water, several sealed snack-packs of cereal bars, cookies, crackers, and raisins. He found travel-sized items such as shaving cream, a disposable razor, toothpaste and a toothbrush, a comb, a bottle of hand-cleanser, a bar of soap, a washcloth, and a thin, flannel-lined wool hat, dyed bright orange. He knew immediately these items had cost his strange benefactor some actual money, and more surprisingly, he understood some real thought went into choosing these items; they were the items a man living on the street needed most.

The homeless man began to cry. He couldn't remember any time in his life on the street when someone had shown him such compassion, or even interest. He felt alive again, instead of the ghost he most often lived as. People who passed him rarely saw him. Those who tossed him coins, or a few bucks, they always avoided his gaze. They shunned him even as they tried to help him with a little cash.

He soon realized, he valued this gift far more than the cold cash the man might have given him. It was the perfect gift: it was just what he needed, exactly when he needed it.

Maybe I'll use the stash to find Alex after all, he thought, *maybe tonight*. He opened the bottle of pain reliever to see it was almost empty. He opened the bottled water, and swallowed the four or five remaining pills, and leaned back against the cold wall of the store behind him. He opened the food packages one by one, savoring them while he waited to see if the medicine would help his throbbing head. As he did, he thought long and hard about his strange benefactor, and what he had said to him in the crowded seconds they spent together.

With his packaged meal finished, he stood, leaning against the wall for balance. To his surprise, his head felt a little better. The throbbing wasn't as bad, even after standing. He turned and walked to an electronics store, only a block away. Before he lost his resolve, he was going to buy a pre-paid cell phone to try to find his son.

Evan's Latest Job

"Have a good day," Evan called after another customer, though he got no response. *They don't even look in my eyes—it's like I'm invisible,* he thought, not for the first time. He never wondered about the lives of *people behind the counter*, before he found himself in their place.

Evan had spent another restless night in which sleep didn't quickly find him. It was another night when he only found rest a few hours before he needed to wake for work. He doesn't hold jobs for very long anymore, and once again, he sensed his boss was about to let him go. He looked out the window behind him, and through the drizzle, he saw the lights of the liquor store on his walk home. His hand began to twitch. *There's no one in the store,* he thought nervously to himself.

Evan was once a confident man. He'd worked in construction, and for ten years, he'd owned his own contracting company. It was small, but he had a role he felt was important. Every day he saw what work he'd accomplished, and he was responsible for the livelihoods of a dozen employees. All that changed with the accident.

He'd sold his business to pay for a lawyer who'd fought hard to keep him out of jail. Some days, he wondered if it was worth it. Standing shift after shift behind the counter of a gas station's convenient mart and deli, had changed his view of the world—it was a darker view indeed.

Debra's Dilemma

"Oh, why didn't I hire a sitter," Debra mumbled as she bit her lip. She knew the answer: she couldn't afford one. She couldn't leave home earlier, without leaving her three young children alone. Waiting for her sister to get off work meant she had no time for traffic, if she was to make her job interview on time.

Being six months out of work meant she had exhausted all her resources. She needed a job soon, or she would be evicted. Her landlord had been more than fair, but she couldn't stay in a house if the utilities were turned off.

Since her husband had died, it hadn't been easy on her and her children, but since she lost her job, she could taste the fear and worry at every trip to the grocery store, and while choosing which bills she would skip each month. This job interview might be the answer to all her prayers. She had applied for a position as secretary at a law firm.

If she was hired, she would have to rely on her mother to watch her kids until she had money to put them in daycare, but she would finally be able to climb out of the debt she'd fallen into. She thought again of her mother, stuck in a job she truly hated since Debra's father left her. Debra once again made a conscious choice not to blame her father for their predicament.

Debra stepped on the brakes, and clenched her teeth as they squealed: another repair she couldn't afford. She saw the traffic slowing at a sign flashing in the rain, *RIGHT LANE ENDS 1000FT.* Traffic crawled nearly to a stop.

No! she protested, nearly heartbroken. *A thousand feet of this? I can't be any later for this interview.*

A desperate idea formed in her mind. *Ooh, I hate it when other people do this,* she thought, as she bit down on her lip even more.

She crowded her car to the right lane, and when all the other cars joined a quarter-mile line to merge, she narrowly passed a row of traffic cones, and rolled past the many, many cars queuing up beside her.

"I hope someone lets me back in," she whispered, both distraught and spent.

Mary's Appointment

Mary was carefully negotiating traffic through a stretch of road construction on her way to the bank. *God, let us get this new loan,* she pleaded silently once again. *So many people will be hurt if we are forced to close.* As an afterthought, she added, *Oh, and Lord? Let my car last another week of driving downtown.*

It was the last of all the banks to which they'd applied; all the others had turned them down. Charitable organizations are not attractive investments during a recession.

The highway narrowed to one lane, and Mary slowed to join a river of taillights where traffic slowed to a crawl as the lanes merged. She spent a long while in traffic before there was any hope of approaching highway speeds again.

She glanced at her watch, and sighed as traffic finally began to pick up speed. To her right, she saw a blue Honda roll by, cutting ahead of a long line of people waiting to merge. Some flashed their lights at her, and several cars honked their horns as the small car passed them. As the car passed Mary, she caught a glimpse of the driver. It was a frenzy-eyed woman in a business suit, glancing desperately to make eye contact with the drivers she passed. Her expression was what Mary noticed first; it was one of anxious fear. No one else was letting her in; the cars in front of, and behind Mary were crowding unreasonably close to keep the blue car from entering traffic again.

"Oh, you poor thing," Mary said under her breath. She nearly stomped on her brakes to make a hole for the woman who seemed so desperate to get ahead in traffic. The cars behind her honked; it was clear to them what Mary was doing.

The woman in the Honda drove desperately for the gap in front of Mary's car. Debra waved excitedly, Mary saw through the Honda's rear window.

Robert's Long Drive

On his way home from the bank, Robert decided to go for a long drive to cool off. His memories tormented him all the way. At his darkest hour, after his wife and daughter's killer was acquitted, he'd vowed to exact his revenge on the object of the most vile hatred he nurtured. The violent intentions snarling within him gathered and focused onto his plan.

He'd followed his family's destroyer from one dead-end job to another. Robert always wore a hat or sunglasses on these late-night trips, but he knew he had little to worry over being recognized. He was a different man, and his appearance had transformed nearly as drastically as his spirit.

He'd devised a plan so filled with hatred, it would have shocked him to hear such an idea only months before. His hatred had spilled past what he held toward his enemy—he had extended it to all of society, who he believed had failed him in denying him justice or revenge. He would strike back at society and his family's killer at once, with this plan he began to long for.

Robert's life was emptied of anything pleasant or desirable, though he didn't merely want to end his own life. To die alone with no one to suffer with him, he felt, would be to accept his enemy's pardon, to ignore the drunk driver's sin.

So he planned. He would end his life, but take his wife's killer with him—and as many innocent bystanders as he could manage.

As his target bounced from job to job, the fifth anniversary of his wife and child's deaths were nearing. The latest job his opponent took was in a public place, even one that would have a small crowd every rush hour. He planned to end his pain on this anniversary.

Since then, he'd abandoned his murderous plan, though his heart held no less hatred for his temporary change. He began spending more time with his relatives—though not those of his deceased wife. To see them again would only throw him into a spiraling depression. He started seeing a grief counselor, and Robert thought it was helping. He began feeling better, and yet the counselor insisted he would find no peace until he learned to replace his hatred with forgiveness.

Time passed as he neared this fated day, and he thought he'd resigned his most violent thoughts for revenge, but in reality, they remained just under the surface, only a single trigger away.

After his rejection at the bank, Robert drove aimlessly, until he found himself in the driveway of his home. He went inside, to wait, to drink, and to try and gather courage.

He opened the box of reminders left from his once-happy family. He hadn't opened the box in years, and he hoped doing so would strengthen his resolve. It did no such thing.

Robert had resigned himself to carry out his horrible plan, though seeing the pictures and belongings of his departed wife had sapped away at his strength. He carefully boxed them up and set them in his car, before returning into his house for an item he had resolved never to use. When he did, he slowly poured out an antique kerosene lamp from his mantel, spilling the contents all over the carpet of his living room. He lit the carpet ablaze, opened a window to feed the flames, stumbled into his car, and drove away.

Sam's Canned Gifts

Sam lost valuable time to a few wrong turns. Instead of hoping he'd get home before rush hour, he began hoping to find the appliance store before it closed. He tried to remember if they closed right at five o'clock, or stayed open later. He knew they closed fairly early, as they did most of their business with professional appliance repairmen, during business hours.

As he turned onto the street where the store was located, he was encouraged, though only briefly. When he read the street address of a building he drove past, he realized he had quite a distance yet to drive.

A nervous-looking woman driving a blue Honda passed him on the right, and he noticed the car seemed lopsided, leaning toward him. He changed lanes to get directly behind it, and saw the rear driver-side tire was nearly flat. The driver hit a pothole, and he thought he heard the rim of the tire strike the pavement. Sam frowned.

That tire won't last long, he thought.

He remembered his rush to the appliance store, and glanced at his watch. He looked ahead on the road and found no pull-offs nearby. The shoulder was pretty narrow, clearly not wide enough to safely change a tire.

He almost decided to pass the car ahead of him and go straight to the store, but he considered what part of town it was—not a great area to stop. He thought of his wife, and how he would feel if she got a flat tire in the same place.

The Honda's right turn signal went on, and Sam saw ahead, the shoulder was somewhat wider. He stepped on the brakes, turned on his blinker, and slowed behind the Honda until they were both stopped. He pulled the trunk-release lever before sliding over to the passenger seat and opening the door. He feared if he opened his driver-side door, the passing traffic might tear it from his car on the narrow shoulder.

It was drizzling, but he approached the passenger-side of the blue car slowly, with both hands raised in a shrugging sort of way. He wanted the woman in the car to see he had nothing in his hands.

Debra rolled the passenger-side window down, only an inch, but said nothing at first. Her eyes were red, as if she'd been crying. She was dressed in a business suit she clearly didn't want to get wet in the rain.

"This just happened," the woman told him desperately, "it wasn't flat only an hour ago."

"Miss, I think I can help. If you pull off a little farther onto the shoulder, I think I can get to your tire and re-inflate it."

"Would you—would you really?" the woman asked in hopeful surprise.

"It will only take a minute or two," he said. "You don't need to get out of your car." He saw a great relief in her eyes. She nodded hurriedly, and pulled forward a little to get farther from the lane of cars flying by them.

Sam walked back to his trunk, and pulled out a tall canister about the size of a can of spray paint. He walked quickly to the rear of the Honda and checked the oncoming traffic.

Lord, watch over me, he prayed silently. His worries for missing the repair shop didn't seem so urgent, while facing so many cars rushing closely past him.

He knelt beside the car's rear tire, hugging himself to the side of the vehicle as cars sped by him. He unscrewed the valve cap and carefully screwed the end of the canister's tiny clear hose onto the valve stem. He pressed the button on the canister and watched as the foamy, sticky contents filled the flat tire.

He dropped the spent can into his trunk, and was about to close it when he paused. Just before he slammed the trunk closed, he grabbed a second tire repair canister, and carried it back to Debra's car. She rolled the passenger window down, with a hopeful look.

"Is it fixed?" she asked, excitedly.

"For now," he said with a smile. "Don't drive too fast, and make sure you take it into a tire shop tomorrow. Oh," he added with a smirk, "warn the guys at the shop the tire was patched with a repair canister. These things can make quite a mess when they remove the valve."

"Oh, *thank* you. I don't know what I would've done if you hadn't stopped." She hesitated, then added, "Surely I need to pay you something."

"No need," he replied, sweeping her suggestion away with a quick motion of his hand. "Take this though." He handed her his last tire repair can. "If it starts to get low again, just screw this on the tire valve and push the button." When he saw her confused look, he added, "It's just like filling a bike tire with a pump. Most likely you won't even need it."

"You carry two of those things?"

"You'd be surprised," he said with a wide grin, "how often these things come in handy. Spend the five bucks and keep one in your trunk, I always say." With that, he tapped the roof of her car with his hand and said, "Drive careful now, ma'am, the roads are pretty slick."

"Wait," she called after him, "What's your name?"

"Sam. If you have to thank someone though, don't thank me—thank God. *He's* the guy who asked me to stop and help you."

"Oh, I will," she yelled after him, smiling, "I surely will."

Tom's New Phone

Tom felt anxious as he entered the electronics store. He took a quick survey of the cramped shop, and was relieved to find no other customers. Other customers meant a higher chance he would be thrown out.

"What do you need?" The store manager couldn't have been more frank.

"I need a cell phone—you know, the kind you pay for up front. I want to call my son."

"Cash?" he responded quickly. The manger seemed to have little patience for Tom.

"Yes," Tom responded, brandishing the bill.

"Is that all you have?"

Tom nodded.

"Okay, wait right here. I'll bring you all the models under a hundred bucks."

Tom shuffled nervously while he waited. He thought of the last time he'd seen his son, and how they'd parted, eight years ago.

He might have had more kids by now, Tom thought to himself. *He could've gotten a divorce and re-married, or…he could be dead.* Tom began to doubt his plan.

"Here they are," said the man when he returned. "These are only twenty bucks, but you have to buy minutes. *These* are fifty, and come with a thousand minutes. This one does too, but it's cheaper, and only works here in the city."

For the first time in nearly a decade, Tom found himself making a financial decision that could have implications further than his most immediate needs. What if he reconciled with his son? What if Alex helped him get back on his feet? Should he choose a phone he would find useful in his new life?

"What about these—why are they so *big*?"

The manager's expression turned worried.

"Those are smart phones. You know: apps, Wi-Fi, videos, internet…"

This sounded unbelievable to Tom. He wondered that he could afford something so amazing.

"Look," the manager said, clearly annoyed. "I'm not going to waste your time being polite. You're living on the street, right?"

Tom reluctantly nodded his head.

"Here's the one you need. It can do some of the smart phone stuff like getting on the internet, but it's rugged, and water resistant. It's only sixty bucks and comes with a thousand minutes. You can bring it to any dealer in the country and buy more minutes later."

Tom picked it up and turned it over. It had some kind of hard rubber padding on all the corners and sides.

"It has Wi-Fi, a five megapixel camera, and—"

"There's a camera inside of it?" Tom asked incredulously. The manager rolled his eyes and turned it on. He pointed the phone at Tom, and snapped a picture.

"There, you see? Come on, old man, we're not getting any younger here."

Tom shifted his eyes to the door, checking for customers.

"Hey, buy it right now, and I'll throw in the charger, free, just to sweeten the deal."

"Sold." Tom couldn't believe he was getting something so fancy for his money. "Wait a minute," he added. "First, prove to me it works—you know, the phone parts. I don't *need* a camera."

The manager made a call using the cell phone, and the phone at the cash register began ringing. He handed the cell phone to Tom. The manager walked quickly to the register and answered the phone.

"Hello. Goodbye." He hung up and walked back to Tom with his hand out, palm facing up. "That's sixty bucks, plus tax."

As he left the store, the manager called after him, "Remember, I said water *resistant*. If you sleep out in the rain much, you're going to break it; no warranty on that."

Tom found a bench and sat down. He pulled the phone out and marveled over it. The last time he used a cell phone, it was nothing like this.

He dialed zero, and pressed *send*. To his surprise, an operator answered.

"Wireless directory services. First lookup is free; second lookup costs you fifty minutes." Tom scolded himself for not knowing how to use the internet features on the phone.

"Um, okay. I need to find my son. His name is Alex Pritcher."

"City, please?" Tom flashed hot with fear. Would Alex have moved away?

"I don't think he moved. Try here—try a local search."

"Two listings. What's his wife's name?"

"Sheryl."

"Okay, I think I found him. I have a home listing, and a cell listing. Which do you want?

"Better give me his cell number," he answered.

"Got it. I'm going to dial the number for you, then you'll have it in your call log. Okay?"

"No, wait! I'm not ready to—" Tom was cut off, and the phone had already dialed.

"Hello, this is Alex. Who's calling, please?"

Robert's Box of Memories

Robert walked quietly from his car, up the sidewalk of a suburban home. When he reached the front door, he silently placed his box of memories on the doormat. When the front porch light came on, it startled him.

Is it motion-sensing? he wondered. *Are they home?*

He heard children's feet running, and a muffled voice through the door.

"It's in, my package came in! I knew it wouldn't take a week."

The door flew open, nearly striking Robert.

"Oh, I hope it's not my package," the young boy said. "It's been opened." His eyes focused on Robert's shoes, and he looked up with a start. "Oh, hi Uncle Bob. Umm…let me get my dad."

Robert's nephew left the door open, and disappeared down the hall. Robert headed for his car. He didn't want a reunion.

"Robert," he heard his brother call out. "Wait—"

"Just dropping that box off, Ricky. I don't want it staring at me anymore," he lied. His brother Richard had a phone to his ear. He quietly asked someone to hold on for a minute.

"Robert, come in and stay—you should be with family today. Why haven't you answered my calls? It's been too long…" Richard turned and took one last look at his brother, stumbling a little as he walked to his car.

"I gotta go. I'm going to set everything straight tonight."

"Robert, have you been drinking?" Richard anxiously asked. "Let me drive you, or call you a cab, at least."

Richard slipped his phone into his pocket, and ran to his departing brother. He could smell the whiskey on his breath.

"Robert—just wait. I have a friend on the phone who's having a bit of an emergency. Just come in and sit down for a minute, will you?"

"No more time, brother, thanks all the same." There was sarcasm in Robert's voice. He got in his car, and drove away.

"Just a minute, Alex," Richard said on the phone. "I'm having a bit of an emergency myself. Let me call you back once I'm on the road, and you can tell me all about it."

Richard ran back inside to grab his cell phone and his keys.

Timothy's Interest

Soon Mary was parking her aging car at the parking garage beside the bank's offices. She pre-paid for the parking slip, and then on her walk from the garage to the office building, she pulled her wallet from her purse, and neatly placed the receipt in it. When she reached the office building, she thought better of it, and pulled the receipt back from her wallet, crumpled it, and dropped it into her large purse.

They can't afford to pay this any more than I can, she thought. She would file no expense report for her drive or parking today.

She reached the bank's receptionist just as her appointment with their loan officer was scheduled to begin.

"You can go right in," the receptionist nearly whispered as she waved toward the door to Timothy's office, "Mr. Dean is waiting for you,"

Mary quietly entered the office, and found Timothy typing at his computer. She opened her mouth to greet him, but he held his index finger up toward her and finished whatever he was typing with the other hand.

"Please sit down," he said when he was finished. "Running a little late, are we?"

Mary checked herself before she replied. She looked into his eyes, and saw something new there. He seemed more *alive* on this day—irritated yes, but also more aware of the world around him.

"Oh, Mr. Dean, I ran into some *awful* traffic, but thankfully, I made it *just* in time," she responded, glancing at her watch.

Timothy looked over his glasses at her, with his nose pointing toward the floor.

"Check your watch," he said in a low monotone.

Mary sat, and pulled from her purse a bundle of papers, rolled up and bound with a hair scrunchy. Timothy's nose twitched. She unbundled them, and laid them flat across her lap. They were all the papers from her correspondence with the bank.

"Thank you for seeing me today," Mary said.

She actually seems thankful, Timothy thought, astonished. *She wouldn't be, if she knew why I first scheduled this meeting.*

He had, in fact, called her back to reject her loan application in person. Once in a while, he gave in to his pettiest whims, and there was something about this woman he did not like. There was no *need* to bring her in to reject the soup kitchen's application—he'd merely *wanted* to.

After his lunchtime experience, however, he felt he couldn't reject the loan so callously. He'd always thought of homeless people as dirty blotches on the face of his fine city. *Not all of them can be worthless wretches,* he'd found himself thinking, *I wouldn't have risked my life to save one of them.*

As he'd waited for Mary's appointment, Timothy reviewed the application once more. He made some phone calls, and performed some internet searches regarding the ministry Mary represented.

The building the ministry operated from was worth double what they owed in their current mortgage, but Timothy already knew this. He'd failed to see before, the property value wasn't included in the original assessment he'd ordered. The property alone was worth several times the value of the building sitting on it.

He found several old newspaper articles about the organization, two of which mentioned Mary. She'd been a volunteer for nearly two decades, and served as an unpaid member of their board of directors for over five years. She was noted by her colleagues as being compassionate and efficient. Her helping hand had nearly transformed a ministry that not only gave soup and temporary shelter to the homeless, but also worked with them to help place them in jobs, help them find them low-rent homes, and find them medical and mental health services when needed.

Timothy realized he not only lacked the capacity to

understand this woman, he also lacked the ability to comprehend any motivation that might have driven her to do such things.

And now, he thought to himself, *here she is, again, in my office.*

"I looked over your application once again," he began. Mary's eyes sparkled with anticipation. "On my second review, it appears I can approve and finalize the refinance you applied for. The terms will be exactly as we discussed before…"

Suddenly, Timothy was struck with a strange noise at such volume, he involuntarily reeled back in horror. Remaining in his chair, he pulled his arms and legs in, nearly into a fetal position at his desk. His eyes sought to find Mary across the desk from him, but she was not there.

"THANK YOU, thank you, thank you, THANK you," Mary yelled excitedly, over and over as she bounded around his desk, shaking his hand until it lifted him from his seat, if such a thing were possible. She threw her arms around him in a great bear hug, and nearly squeezed the breath out of him.

"I can't *tell* you how much this *means* to me—all of us at as the shelter," she cried, still clutching him to her. The door to the office swung wildly open, and a security guard, followed closely by the bank's receptionist, burst into the room. They were not prepared for the sight before them.

Timothy's arms flapped limply over Mary's shoulders, as she was apparently trying to cling onto him and jump for joy at the same time.

The receptionist turned away, her face twisted in empathetic embarrassment. The security guard looked as if he might draw his sidearm, his face covered in the ultimate expression of uncertainty.

"Are you—are you all right, sir?" The guard stammered. Timothy didn't immediately respond.

Mary finally deposited Timothy onto his seat, then closed the gap between herself and the guard in two quick steps, grasping him in embrace. If she'd moved any slower, the guard might have interpreted her affections as an attack, but she was altogether too fast for him.

Mary showered them all with another round of heartfelt thanks, which were just as sincere as they were unwelcome. When she turned to grasp the receptionist and hug her as well, she squeaked out a nearly inaudible, "You're welcome," and darted from the room at a surprising pace.

As she walked from the bank to the parking garage, newly signed papers bound in a tightly-clutched envelope, she cast her gaze to the clouds overhead, and whispered her most profound and warmest thanks.

Once in her car, she told herself merrily, "I'm going to treat myself to a snack on my way back to the office." The workday was nearly over, but her work on this day was not yet finished.

Debra's Interview

Debra found a parking spot at the address from the email she received concerning her interview. It was in a large business park in the downtown area, with many newly-erected buildings.

She found the building number easily enough, with a few minutes to spare to fix her makeup. It had been an arduous drive.

Thank you, Lord, she prayed, casting her eyes skyward.

When she found the correct office, she nearly lost her breath. *Steele Legal Recruiting & Staffing, LTD,* was written in large gold letters over the doorway.

Dear God—not a staffing agency. She was led to believe she was interviewing for an actual job. An agency could take months to find her temporary work, even if they loved her.

Nervously, she walked inside and greeted the receptionist.

"Miss O'Brien will see you in just a moment."

Debra knew they had scheduled her interview late, but she began to worry when she saw no other candidates.

A tall, slender woman in a striped business suit entered the reception area from an adjacent conference room.

"Miss O'Brien?" Debra asked, as she stood to greet her interviewer.

"Thank goodness you made it," she responded excitedly. "Just follow me through here. We'll get started right away."

The woman asked Debra if she would like anything to drink, and she politely refused.

"There is one thing you could clarify for me," Debra suggested. "When I scheduled this interview, I was told it was with the law firm where I'd applied—not a staffing agency."

"Oh, yes," her interviewer responded. "The Davis firm is under contract with our agency. They do all their staffing through us." When Debra didn't seem satisfied, she added, "This is an interview for immediate placement in Davis—we need someone to start on Monday."

Debra drew a deep breath, and exhaled in relief. She was focused. The rest of the short interview went well, and both ladies knew it.

"If you're prepared to sign papers tonight," the interviewer said as she drew the interview to a close, "I can extend a signing bonus to you."

"Really?" Debra asked suspiciously. "And what about compensation?" She bit her cheek to keep from smiling. *A signing bonus?*

"At the top of the range listed in your packet from Davis. We're scrambling to fill positions for their new office."

On her way to her car, Debra could hardly keep herself from screaming for joy. She had no idea the firm where she'd applied was opening a new office—which just happened to be thirty minutes closer to her home. Signing bonus in hand, she could hire sitters until she could arrange for her children's day care. *With this job,* she thought of her new pay, *Mom can finally quit, and watch the kids at home if she wants.*

She began her drive home elated, knowing nothing of the surprise awaiting her just a few miles away.

A Desperate Call

Richard had to speed to catch up with his brother's old sedan.

What is he planning? he wondered. *He sounded so—final.*

He followed him all the way downtown, losing him several times in the process. While he was caught in traffic, he took the time to call his friend, Alex.

"Alex? Richard here. I'm sorry I had to hang up on you like that. I'm having a bit of a family emergency, too." Richard explained the situation to his friend.

"It's wonderful you heard from your father, especially after all this time," Richard changed the subject back to Alex's problem. "I'm sorry you're out of town. How far out are you?"

"Out of state, visiting my in-laws. We're packing up, getting ready to head out, but it'll be a few hours, at least. Look, I feel for you and what your brother's going through, I just don't have anywhere else to turn."

"You said he called you from a cell phone?"

"Some no-brand thing he picked up in the city," Alex replied. "It doesn't have caller-ID enabled. I still can't believe he *called*. He hung up when he started crying, and hasn't called back. He didn't even stay on the phone long enough for me to tell him we're out of town. This is what has me going crazy, Richard: *he gave me an ultimatum.* He said if I can forgive him for walking out on us when I was a kid, I need to meet him at some corner downtown, in less than an hour."

Richard heard the concern in his friend's voice. "These things always happen for a reason. Why don't we pray about it together?" Alex found this a prudent idea.

"Dear Jesus, we both come to you with heavy hearts tonight. We're afraid for our families. We ask you humbly, bring Alex's father safely home to him tonight. Let me catch up to Robert, before it's too late. Keep him from hurting anyone, *please*. Keep him from…" Richard's throat caught, and he fell silent. Alex completed his thought for him, and waited silently for him.

"Oh, God," Richard finally called out, "he's exiting the highway."

Sam's Late Arrival

The traffic grew thicker, and Sam realized he shouldn't have taken the busy road along its full length—there had to be a faster path to the store.

I might as well go home, he thought, *it's already after five.* He knew he was nearly there, and so he risked a little more time in rush hour traffic to see his drive to its end. *If I have to come back, at least I'll know exactly where it is.*

Finally, he found his destination. The sign was lit, *Tony's Appliance Repair and Supply*, though the lights inside were dim. There were still a few cars in the parking lot, but they looked as if they might have been there for months.

He got out of his car and checked the front door, just in case. It was locked. He yelled out in a burst of anger, *"Come on!"*

He grumbled to himself as he got back on the highway, and turned back the way he'd come.

Dark Clouds

Evan's mood hadn't improved; in fact he was feeling worse than usual. He dreaded this day each year; the anniversary of the worst day of his life. He only wanted it end.

The next customer bought a blueberry muffin and coffee. She seemed to take an immense amount of pleasure, choosing creams and flavorings for her coffee. When she brought her food to the counter, Evan could see she was beaming with joy. She looked him directly in the eye, and asked how his day was.

"Wha—what?" Evan stammered in surprise.

"I'm Mary," she went on. "How's your day going…Evan?" She read his name from the badge pinned to his shirt.

"Well, all right, I suppose." Evan hardly knew what to say.

"Isn't it usually busier in here?" she asked.

"Guess it's the rain," Evan responded, noncommittally. "It does seem strange, though," he added.

Evan and Mary didn't know it, but there *were* strange circumstances involved. The store should be full of people on their way home from work, grabbing something to eat, or a coffee, or a soda. The people who normally would have been in the store were each of them delayed, somehow kept away from the store that night.

One man had caught the flu, and had to miss his shift at work, though he badly needed the money.

Another was running late because he broke his expensive watch, and didn't realize until too late, he had stayed an extra hour in the office.

One of the store's most regular customers, a kindly single mom, had recently had surgery on her foot. Her slowed pace had cost her a place on the bus she'd meant to catch.

Another man had just been laid off from work, and was consumed with why his boss had chosen him. Had he gone to work, he would have stopped at the store, like on most nights, for a soda and snack on his long drive home.

All these people, and many more, would have been at this store at this very moment, but for some twist of fate.

Just then, the screeching sound of skidding tires pulled Mary's and Evan's gazes through the window behind the counter, to the parking spaces at the storefront. A dark sedan slid into the front panel of an older model car that had seen better days.

"Oh no, my car!" Mary cried, as her hands flew to her mouth in surprise.

"What is going on out there?" Evan said angrily.

A confused, middle-aged man hastily threw open his car door, hitting the yellow safety pole near the curb. The man was walking strangely, with something in his hand. He threw a pint bottle at the glass storefront. The bottle shattered, sending whiskey splattering across the window, even as it spider-webbed the window's glass from corner to corner.

"Hey," Evan yelled, "you can't do that—*I'm calling the police!*" The strange man reached into his jacket pocket and pulled something from it with an awkward, jerky motion.

Robert lumbered into the store, while Mary stumbled backward onto a cardboard display of candy bars. Robert squared himself as best as he could, facing Evan with all the fury and pain of the past five years evident in his eyes.

Evan's eyes were drawn to the man's right hand, as he raised it to shoulder-height, brandishing a shiny pistol.

Debra's Doubts

While she drove through downtown, Debra called her mother and shared her good news. Debra's mother was even happier than she had been.

"Let's all go out to dinner tonight," her mother suggested, "it will be my treat."

"Oh, I'd love to Mom, but I'm going to be a while. I'll be in rush-hour traffic the entire way."

"I'll relieve your sister, and feed the kids something light. If you get home in time, we can still go out."

"That sounds great. Thank you."

"Thank *God*," her mother reminded her.

Debra smiled. "Yes, I know, Mom." It did her heart well to hear her mother so joyful. Ever since her father left them, her spirits were rarely so high.

After she ended her call, she decided to leave the highway and take another path, using the surface roads through downtown. Guilt still lingered from her quarter-mile shortcut she took while she struggled to get to her interview on time.

She found the surface roads just as backed up. When traffic ground to a halt, she began scanning the cross streets, wondering if she could find a faster route. Finally, she saw traffic speeding up after a traffic light ahead.

As she crossed the intersection, she saw the red plastic of a tail light, and clear glass from someone's head lights from the minor accident Robert caused when he ran through the same intersection, earlier that day. She bit her lip and sucked air in through her teeth as she heard a piece *crunch* beneath her tires. She fondly remembered her flat-tire-rescuer, and looked at the tire repair can beside her on the seat. She'd never heard of such a thing before.

She hit her left turn signal when she saw the cause for the delay in the lane ahead of her. There was a long, black luxury car at a full stop, just a few cars in front of her. She just began to change lanes to drive around it when she realized what she was doing.

Some stranger just saved my interview by stopping to help me, she thought. *How can I pass this car without so much as a thought for whoever's inside?*

She looked at the businesses on the both sides of the street. *It's not a nice part of town,* she reasoned with herself. *If I were a man, it would be different.* Still she hesitated, now immediately behind the car causing the delay. She saw its rear passenger tire was completely flat.

It's not dark yet, her thoughts continued. *There are plenty of people around, watching—plenty of witnesses.* In the end, her word choice convinced her. A *witness* is exactly what she desired to be; a Good Samaritan. She chuckled at herself for not seeing the obvious pun, after she'd just been helped by a stranger named *Sam*.

Debra pulled all the way to the curb, just behind the black car. To be safe, she slid over and climbed out of her car on the passenger side, away from traffic. She brought the new tire repair can her own personal Good Samaritan had given her.

As she approached the passenger side of the car, Timothy rolled down the window, and, clearly flustered, kept his gaze on his phone while he madly punched at it with his finger. He began, "I have no service here. I can't make any calls at all!"

Debra was at a loss for words. She stood there, craning down to Timothy's open window, and said nothing. Finally, the man looked up and gave her his attention.

"I will pay you handsomely, if I could only use your…" He abruptly stopped, eyes locked on Debra's face. He too, was visibly shocked. *"Debby? Is that you?"*

Debra's jaw clamped tightly closed. Through clenched teeth, she responded, *"Yes, Dad,* it is."

Sam's Sudden Change of Attitude

Sam was still angry on his way home. As he drove, his anger was slowly replaced by a strange scene forming in his mind. He imagined watching the news that night, and seeing a reporter standing under an umbrella, reporting a traffic accident. A woman driving a blue Honda had died on the side of the road, trying to change a tire in the rain. In his mind's eye, he recognized the car behind the reporter, and the location of the car. It was exactly where he stopped to help her, the location he had seen her safely drive away from after he inflated her tire.

"All right, God," he said, still half-wondering whether or not the scene in his mind was imagined, "I get it—it was worth the trip."

His anger was gone, and he felt a great well of peace in his heart. He saw a convenience store with a gas station up ahead, and chuckled to himself.

Keep one in the trunk, I always say. He turned on his blinker and pulled into the store's parking lot, not willing to wait another day to replace the repair canisters he'd just given away.

He decided to fill his gas tank before he entered into the convenience store, and noticed it had a deli inside.

Might as well get some dinner, he thought, *and miss a little rush hour traffic.*

Sam called his wife, and explained why he would miss dinner.

"*Oh, no,*" she consoled him. "You took a half-day off from work to pick up the part you needed. Now you'll have to do the whole thing over again on another day."

"Oh, it's all right," he added. "I have a feeling God's trying to show me something. I'll tell you all about it when I get home."

Once he got off the phone, he heard the gas pump clunk off; his tank was full. While he paid, he noticed a car parked crooked, right across a handicap spot. He left his car at the pump, and began walking to the small store. He saw the smashed window, and quickened his pace.

Out of Power

Alex remained silent, waiting to hear what Richard next had to say. Richard pulled onto the shoulder of the highway, and followed it the last hundred yards to the exit ramp. When he followed his brother through a right turn at the next traffic light, he carelessly hit the curb with both tires on the passenger side, nearly causing him to drop his phone to the floor.

"Listen, Alex, I need to hang up. I just hit a

curb…he's driving erratically—whoa, I lost him! I'll call you back just as soon as I can; I *have to find him.* Text me the address where your father said to meet him."

Richard drove desperately around the block, scanning every car he passed. When he didn't find him, he chose the next block, and circled it, too. Halfway around the block, he heard the out-of-battery signal from his cell phone as it powered itself off. He chided himself for leaving the car-charger in his wife's car.

Just when he was about to turn back on his tracks and search both blocks again, he saw the dark outline of his brother's car, half-blocking the handicap spot at a gas station's convenient mart. He gunned the engine, and screeched to a halt at the far end from the entrance.

No Coincidences

Debra hadn't spoken to her father for years. She long thought she would *never* speak to him again. After he left her mother, after he'd weaseled out of alimony and child support, she had hated him for a long time. She bit her tongue to guard against saying those things she'd so dearly wanted to say to him in anger.

Timothy looked at the canister Debra still held in her hand, and she saw a thought register in his mind. *You're here to help me,* his eyes seemed to say.

He must know I have no idea what kind of car he drives, after so long, Debra thought. *He knows I approached him as a stranger.*

She guessed he might turn his face from her, ask her to leave, or accuse her of some imagined slight, but the reaction he showed her instead, she had no way of predicting.

Timothy buried his face in his hands, and began to cry. She'd never seen him cry. When he stopped, he leaned across the passenger seat, and opened the door.

"I'm so sorry, Debra. *Please,* please come in and sit down. I have so much to tell you."

She did, and they began a long, meaningful conversation—one that would take much time, and faith, and trust to work out, but it was also one that convinced Debra her father was broken, he was at the cusp of becoming a changed man.

"Dad," she said before long, "we have to get our cars out of the road—we're blocking traffic."

Timothy's eyes widened. He seemed to have completely forgotten he was parked in the right lane of a busy road.

"Over there, Dad, only a block down, on the right. Just drive slowly on your flat tire, and park right there." Wagging the tire repair can, she added, "I'll follow in my car and fill your flat for you."

He agreed, and soon they were sitting and talking in her car, in the nearly-empty parking lot of a convenience store that was normally quite busy during rush hour.

Robert's Untimely and Horrific End

Just inside the front door of the convenience mart, Robert leveled the pistol at Evan's head, vile thoughts flying confusingly through his mind. Evan fell half-a-step backward, and threw his hands in the air.

"Don't shoot—I'll open the cash register," Evan shouted, squinting his eyes against his attacker, as if his eyelids could shield him from such violent intentions. Then, something clearly registered in Evan's mind. "Wait—*I know you*. You've been in here before, skulking around, wearing dark shades." With a horrifying flash of recognition, Evan's eyes opened wide. "Today's the anniversary—and you're her husband."

After five hellish years without them, Robert thought, *I'm finally doing it.* Robert was shaking with anger, though the end of his firearm remained fixed, centered on Evan's head.

Mary found herself rousing to consciousness in a most

uncomfortable position. She couldn't sit up, bent over backward on a nearly-destroyed cardboard display of chocolate bars. With a tiny groan, she rolled past a tall display of sunglasses, and struggled to sit up. Her eyes grew wide, and she peered carefully past the sunglasses case. She found Robert screaming at the cashier, a handgun leveled at the cashier's head.

"Tell me you don't deserve it!" Robert demanded. When he received no response, he shouted it again, louder.

The cashier's chin quivered like a child's as he responded in near-silence.

"I…I can't."

Robert was all the more enraged. He swung wildly, knocking a countertop display of lottery tickets from beside the cash register. His pistol cracked the clear plastic display open, cutting his hand.

"You KNOW you deserve death—you admit it!"

Evan let out a stifled sob, finally sputtering out his response.

"Of course I know it—*I killed them*." He began sobbing loudly, no longer holding back his fear and anger and unforgiveness, and shame. "I haven't had a single night's sleep since the crash. You think I escaped prison, but I didn't—I live in the prison of my soul. Dying can't be any worse."

Robert's eyes grew wide, and he reacted as if he'd been slapped hard in the face. He found a common hatred with his wife's killer—the hatred he held for himself. This brought Robert no solace, and earned Evan no pardon.

Mary took this horrific moment to stand and call out, "Mister, you don't want to do this. Please, put down your gun."

Robert instead trained his pistol on Mary, ready to fire. Mary let out a tiny scream.

"What?" Evan reacted, "You're going to kill *her*, too? She did nothing! Why murder her? She never harmed you."

Robert stumbled back a half-step, nearly to the front

door. He waivered. He trained his gun once again on Mary.

"Take me, but leave her," Evan said. "Let me do something right, let me help someone. Let it be because of me that she gets to go home to her family tonight."

This struck Robert unimaginably hard. He saw through another perspective, briefly, from a point of view outside himself. He saw himself as the killer, robbing another man of his wife. He should've seen this in his motives long ago, but he was as blinded by hatred as people seldom are. His hatred turned onto himself—it wasn't a long transition from the pity and shame he'd lived in for the past few years. He let his arm follow his hatred, aimed solely at himself, and finished the task he'd begun so long ago, in destroying his own life.

Mary screamed aloud at the gunshot, and did a frantic little frightened-by-a-mouse kind of dance. She ran to Evan, though he was a stranger to her, and held on to him tightly. Evan put his arm around her and let her bury her face in his shoulder.

Tragedy's Sometimes Beautiful Aftermath

Before long, Evan could no longer hold Mary up. In fact, he found he couldn't even stand. He released her, then fell clumsily to the floor. He had lost all hope.

"What's wrong?" Mary asked, frantically. "Were you hit?" she asked, though she'd clearly seen he wasn't.

"I *wanted* him to kill me. I killed his family—crashed into them, driving drunk, five years ago today. I don't want to live."

Mary grabbed him by the head, stared directly into his eyes, and, drawing on an inner strength she'd never felt so powerfully, spoke fierce truths to him.

"Don't you give up on me! God has a plan for you yet, son. You watch and see, he has a plan for you to live, and wants to see you walk in forgiveness."

Evan seemed at first to acknowledge her, but then withdrew. Mary recognized the symptoms of shock in him, and worked to comfort him.

"Don't you worry," she said, as she propped him up against the door. "The police will be here soon. I'll stay right here and wait with you." Her eyes fell on Robert's body, and she bit down on her tongue to fight back the retching in her throat.

"Let's wait outside for them," she told Evan, matter-of-factly. "We don't want to be in the police's way when they get here."

Mary pulled at Evan's arm as she tried to lift him from the floor. He followed her cues in a daze. She sat him down on a long bench directly outside the shop's door, across the sidewalk from her battered car. Mary sat down beside him.

Richard ran from his car, to the front of the small store. He was about to run inside, when a woman approached him from the bench beside the door. He hadn't even noticed her until she spoke.

"Richard!" Mary called, "Thank God you're here. Wait—why *are* you here?" Confused, Richard tried to sidestep her.

"I have to find my brother—I think he went in…" His gaze bounced back and forth between the store's entrance, and his friend Mary. "Wait, what are *you* doing here?"

"It's a long story," she said as she put her hand flat against his chest. "Richard, you don't want to go in there. We're waiting for the police."

"The police?" Richard responded. "I have to find my brother—I think he went in this store." He froze for a moment, afraid of what he might find inside. "Why are the police coming?"

"Oh, dear Lord," Mary squeaked. She stood on her toes to whisper in Richard's ear. Richard bolted through the door. Mary sat back down beside Evan, who was still very much in shock.

A homeless man wearing a new, bright orange hat walked by, his head cast down.

"Why didn't I stay on the phone longer?" he mumbled. "Why don't I call him back?" Tom had little hope left in his eyes. He'd reached the gas station, but it brought no happiness to him.

"Sir, you can't go in there," Mary said to Tom, as he tried to enter the store.

"Oh, did they go out of business?" Tom asked.

"No, there's been…a crime inside. We're waiting for the police." Mary approached the man. She saw his clothes, his scruffy beard, and she immediately recognized him as a man living on the streets. "Sir, what can I do for you?"

"Nothing. I'm waiting here for my son. Mind if I sit?" he asked, half-expecting her to refuse him. She shook her head with a warm smile, and Tom joined her on the bench.

Sam's attention was on the store's entrance. He wore a curious expression, but remained beside his car, at the gas pump. He stood tentatively, as if he were considering asking the people what had happened.

Soon Richard came out from the store, crying. He sat beside Tom on the bench, which was growing increasingly crowded. Mary stood and laid her arm on Richard's shoulder.

"That was your brother?" she asked.

"Yes," he replied in a whisper. "Did he—" he started, in a pained voice, "did he harm anyone else?"

"No, only himself. It seems he wanted to, but…I think we talked him out of it."

"Well, thank God for that," he said, tearfully. He buried his face in his hands for a few moments, then looked up in surprise.

"I forgot to call him back! Mary, do you have a cell phone on you?"

"No, I'm afraid I left it at home."

"Do you?" Richard turned to Evan, who was still in shock.

"Don't own one," Evan answered in a monotone.

Richard looked at last to Tom, who looked quite despaired.

Richard grimaced as he asked Tom, "Sir, do you have a cell phone? I have a very urgent call to make."

Tom jerked a little before he reacted. "Yes I do! I have a cell phone."

Richard pleaded with him anxiously, "May I use it for a quick call? I'd gladly pay you."

"Have a go at it," Tom replied, proudly handing Richard his new phone.

Fortunately, Richard knew Alex's cell number. He dialed him up, to hear Alex answer in excited tones.

"Is this—is it you Dad? Are you there?"

"No, Alex, this is Richard. I just borrowed a stranger's phone—my battery died.

"Oh. I saw the caller-ID was blocked, and hoped it was him. We're on our way now."

"What's the address of the place where you need to meet your father?" Richard asked. Tom's ears perked up. "Corner of Fifth and Vine, okay; near the gas station." Richard put his hand over the cell phone, and asked, "Do any of you know where Fifth and Vine is?"

Evan seemed to snap out of his daze for a moment. "You're sitting on it, pal."

"What?" Richard asked. "That's odd. Now Alex, how will I recognize him? *Really?*" Richard leaned toward Tom, staring at his orange hat, and asked, "Is your name...*Tom?*"

"Yes, it is. Who are you talking to?" Tom asked excitedly.

Richard was shaken. "Uh, I think it's your son...Alex?" he finished questioningly. When he saw Tom's expression, he added, "Sir, your son is driving back to town just as fast as he can right now, to come and find you. He asked me to wait with you while he drives here. He's very worried about you."

At that, Richard handed Tom's phone back to him. Tom stood and leaned against the wall, mostly listening to his son on his brand new cell phone, tears streaming down his face.

"I was afraid you wouldn't come...I thought you didn't want to see me..."

Timothy and his daughter were still talking in Debra's car, when Tom first arrived, moments ago.

"That's the hobo who saved me!" he exclaimed to his daughter.

"The man on the corner, who pulled you from the bus?"

"Yes, the same man, I'm sure of it. I should do something, I should thank him..."

The two of them spoke while Timothy gathered his courage.

"Would you go with me?" he asked his daughter. "It's not a bad area, really; I stop here quite often." Debra only nodded, though she smiled warmly when she eyed her father.

"You really have changed," she told her father softly.

The two of them walked up to the store front, and Timothy pointed to Tom.

"Yes, I'm certain this is him," Timothy told his daughter. As he and his daughter approached the store front, he saw Tom returning his cell phone to his pocket.

"What are you doing here?" Timothy asked.

Richard interjected protectively, "Can I help you sir? This man is a new friend of mine."

"This man saved my life today," Timothy cried, "and I didn't even take the time to thank him."

Cautiously, Tom responded, "I'm about to meet my son. I haven't seen him in years." Tom smiled wide and quietly added, "I want to get off the streets now." Timothy's eyes grew wide.

"You're being reunited with your son?" Timothy

exclaimed. He flashed a smile at his daughter. "Well, it won't do to meet him like this!"

Timothy pulled off his overcoat and put it around Tom's shoulders, then pulled off his hat, and placed it over Tom's orange hat. He looked back to Richard, and asked him, "Are you truly this man's friend?"

Richard nodded, confused.

"Here, take this; use it to help him," Timothy insisted, pulling a wad of cash from his front pocket, and handing it to Richard. "It's the least I could do."

Mary seemed to wake from some distant thought, as she recognized Timothy, with his coat and hat removed.

"Mr. *Dean?*" she exclaimed. *"What are you doing here?"*

Alarmed once again by her volume, Timothy involuntarily took a step back. Debra couldn't help letting out a chuckle.

"It's *me,* Mr. Dean, from the bank. You just approved the shelter's loan today. I was in your office, only an hour or two ago."

Timothy smiled wide. "I suppose you were. How can this be?" When no one spoke, he added, "I suppose it's not all that unlikely. In fact, I was going to stop here to get some dinner from the deli, before my tire went flat. I ran over some glass in the road, it seems. But what are *you* doing here?"

"Oh, I stopped on the way home, too. I'm glad I did, because I met a new friend here, named Evan. He's had a pretty rough night." Evan seemed to nod slightly, still in shock. "And a friend of mine from church, Richard Stevens just happened to be here also." She pointed to Richard, who tried to nod and smile, but didn't quite have the heart for it.

"Stevens, you say?" Timothy asked. "You look familiar. While we're chalking up coincidences, you don't happen to be related to a Robert Stevens, do you?"

Richard turned away momentarily, lost in grief for his brother. He would stand at a distance, watching over Tom until the police and his friend Alex arrived.

Timothy soon learned if he hadn't had a flat tire, not

only would he not have been reunited with his daughter, but he very likely would have been in the store when Richard entered. Timothy was certain Robert would have shot him—the bank manager who'd denied his loan only hours earlier. This knowledge humbled Timothy greatly, later forcing him to take a slightly more introspective look at his life.

Debra finally noticed the man who'd fixed her tire, standing at a comfortable distance.

"Sam!" she cried out. He looked back at her, pointing to himself. "Dad, this is the man I just told *you* about—the man who fixed my tire, so I could get to my job interview. He's the reason I stopped to help you when I saw your car had a flat."

"Oh, indeed?" Timothy asked, taken aback once again.

These people, all touched in an unforgettable way—some through horror and loss, but all, though something special and life-changing—stood there outside the convenience store, sharing their lives with one another. It would be a long, long while before any of them forgot what each had experienced that day. A friendly look, a patient moment of compassion, a word, or even a helpful act spent in hope, had changed more than any of them could have guessed. When we are hurt, and in turn, hurt others, it's not only our hearts here on Earth we grieve, but also, God's breaking heart in heaven.

Note from the Author

In life, our every action causes a reaction, but it is rarely opposite or equal. Any single action you make, if it could affect two people in such a way that they each do the same for two others, would grow at an exponential rate. This means, if each following reaction happened within two hours, your original action could potentially affect all of earth's seven billion people in less than three days.

Imagine that; a single decision you make could theoretically affect every inhabitant of our planet in a personal way, in less than three days. This isn't going to happen, but just as this story illustrates, this fact shows you can affect many, many people with how you choose to react to others.

The next time someone wrongs you, remember:

The guy in the store who was rude to you—that was Robert, the man who violently lost his family and is contemplating suicide.

The person who cut you off on the highway—that was Debra, the single mom who's out of work and late to interview for a job she desperately needs.

The coworker who talks about you behind your back—that's Timothy. Abused as a child, Timothy lost his ability to place trust in others at an early age, and he began striking out at others in anonymous ways. It led him to destroy his every relationship, until he became a lonely, bitter man, too caught up in his cycle of causing and receiving pain to reach out to others, or to call his only child to reconcile their past.

Many people hurting others were first hurt themselves, and haven't yet come to terms with their pain or learned to release it through forgiveness.

I believe there are *acts of kindness*, acts of blessing

others, that God has in store for you, and there's nothing random about them. They are orchestrated to affect those around you. They may affect untold numbers of people. We pass them up every day, and sometimes, we meet these opportunities with all the love God placed within us, and they work spectacular results—chain reactions we will never see.

Some of them are spontaneous—a word or a question, a sincere sign of concern—while others may take preparation, like our Good Samaritan, Sam, who stays up late once a month, making the care packs he keeps in his car, so he can hand them out whenever he runs into someone in need.

Listening for, and following God's quiet promptings is anything but random. Random acts have random results, but God's work in people's lives is transformative, miraculous, and has eternal significance. I ask of you, dear reader, consider this carefully when you next meet a stranger. You cannot fathom the positive effect your words and actions may have— not only on these strangers, but on untold numbers of others.

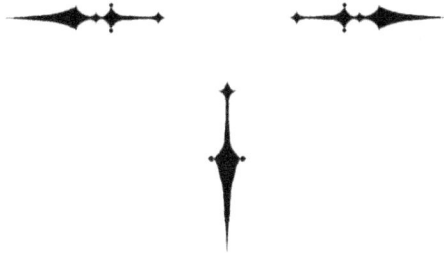

Wi-Fi® is a registered trademark of Wi-Fi Alliance.
Honda is a registered trademark of American Honda Motor Company, Inc.

Chris M. Hibbard

In God's Eyes

He was caught in traffic, wondering why the red light ahead of him was keeping him from his family, on one of the shortest days of the year. His mind was troubled. His eldest son, ever vibrant and filled with joy, had seemed so somber lately—and the burden of knowledge weighed heavily on this father. His cell phone buzzed, and his foot nearly slid off the brake as he fished it out of his pocket. It was his wife.

"I'm on my way," he answered the phone. "Is Johnny home from school yet?"

"Yes, he is," his wife replied. There was pain in her voice, the deep concern of a loving mother. After a brief pause, she went on. "It happened again."

His face flushed with anger, and he found himself clenching his teeth, even holding his breath.

"I'll be there as soon as I can. I love you."

Why God? he demanded as he hung up. *Why do you let this happen?*

When he pulled into the driveway, he noticed the walkway to the front door had a fresh coat of snow. *Time to shovel the walk again.* He *crunch-crunched* his way inside, and stomped the snow from his shoes. He passed his two youngest children in the living room, playing video games.

"Hey, Dad."

"Hi, Daddy!"

"Hey guys. Is your homework finished?" He tousled their hair on his way through the living room.

"Yep."

"Almost…"

He smiled. He rounded the corner into the kitchen and found his wife standing at the counter, nervously flipping through a magazine. Her body was rigid with pent-up frustration. He embraced her from behind, and craned his neck to kiss her cheek. As he did, his lips met with a salty tear. He squeezed her tight.

"Is he in his room?"

"In the bathroom," she replied. "He won't come out."

He made his way down the hall, and knocked on the bathroom door.

"*Occupied*," he heard Johnny's voice on the other side of the door."

"I'm home," his father said tentatively. It was almost a question. *Do you want to talk?*

"I'm *busy*," Johnny answered. His voice nearly cracked.

"Okay. Come out for dinner when you're ready."

He returned to the kitchen and sat down. His wife's Bible still lay there from earlier in the day, across the table from him. Almost as an afterthought, he reached for it, and spun it around so he could read it. It was opened to Psalms 56, and he found not a few notes scribbled in the margin near verses eight and nine. One note read: *Lord, hear me cry,* and another, *watch over our family.*

Soon, the table was set, and dinner was served.

"Kids," his wife called loudly, "it's time to eat."

Johnny was last to come to the table. He held a washcloth half-filled with melting ice cubes to the corner of his mouth. His cheek was red and swollen.

"It's your favorite, Johnny," his mother said cheerfully, "beef stew." All day she'd looked forward to seeing his smile at dinner. She'd been praying for him from the time she started the beef stock in the morning, until she turned the stove off that evening. The house was filled with the warm aroma, but it brought no smile to Johnny.

"Why is his face still *red?*" his youngest sibling asked, pointing.

"Never mind," their mother answered. "Eat your salad, honey. Don't spill your stew."

It was a quiet meal. Johnny's father missed his son's rambunctious stories from his day at school. When dinner was over, Johnny cleared the table silently, and went directly to his room.

"No games...no videos?" his father asked him. He only shook his head in response. His father followed him into his room and sat beside him on the edge of his bed. "Son, tell me what happened."

Johnny looked about to answer, then turned away as his eyes squinted out fresh tears. He dropped his gaze to the floor.

"I tried, Dad, I really *tried.*"

His mind raced. Had he tried to fight back—or tried to avoid the bully altogether?

"You tried *what*, Son?" he asked, cautiously.

"I tried *praying*...but nothing happened. He still found me, and he still beat me up." As he spoke, his expression changed from desperation to shame.

"It's not your fault, Johnny. Bullies...just want to bully people." He cringed even as he said it. *Can't I come up with something better than that?* He sighed. "I don't know what to say, Johnny." He wrapped an arm around him and patted his shoulder. "Can I pray along with you?"

"Okay," he mumbled. "You start."

Johnny's father slid to his knees, and placed his elbows on the bed. Johnny knelt beside him, waiting. His father searched for something comforting, but he felt only anger. With another sigh, he began.

"God, come hear us tonight. Hear our prayer and answer it." He faltered, wanting to shield his son from the rage building inside him. Knowing he'd rather be honest than appear right, he finally blurted out, "God, *protect my son!*" He prayed the bully would be caught and punished. He prayed the other boys at school would also stand up to him, or if not, at least report him to the principal—something Johnny wasn't willing to do.

When they were finished, he hugged his son tightly, and told him how proud of him he was. "There's nothing wrong about reporting him, Johnny," he told him yet again. His son only shook his head.

"It will only get worse, Dad."

He told his son he wanted to talk to his principal, just to ask him to assign an aid outside to watch over the children before and after school. Again, Johnny refused. He left his son's room feeling worse than when he'd followed him in.

Back in the kitchen, Johnny's mother was praying also. As she heard her husband approach, she rose from the table, then leaned against his chest. He saw the Bible on the table; she'd turned to another scripture, and she'd been writing on a notepad beside it.

"It *will* get better, hon. I just wish you'd let me speak to the school," she told him.

He searched for a response, but he had no words to bring her comfort.

"I feel so helpless," he finally replied, clearly frustrated. "There's *nothing* I can *do*." He pulled away from her, and reached for his jacket.

"Where are you going?" his wife asked.

"For a walk." He winced to think his anger was only going to add to his wife's concerns. He needed some time to calm down. On his way past the table, his eye caught on the words his wife had written on the ruled lines of her notepad.

Ps 68:5-6a: *Take away his anger Lord, let him see*

Unwilling to be swayed by words, he stormed out the back door. Unwittingly, he'd stepped right into a snow drift.

Oh, great, he thought as he stomped through a fresh foot of snow, heading for the driveway. It had cooled considerably since he'd returned home. As the snow pushed up his pant legs, he could feel it clinging in clumps to his socks. He reached the street and started walking aimlessly. It was so silent, every noise trapped by the fresh blanket of snow. It was a clear night, and he could see the constellations overhead. The air had the smell of a cold winter night. His steps crunched on the snow left on the road after it had been plowed.

He pulled a wool cap from the pocket of his jacket and pulled it over his head. *It's supposed to get down to zero tonight,* he remembered. He reached into the other pockets of his thick jacket to pull out his gloves. His hand found something else, something he'd all but forgotten. Earlier that day, when he went to pay his bill at the cafe where he'd eaten lunch, he found a small rack of MP3 players beside the cash register. He'd waved his hand questioningly toward them, and the cashier smiled.

"Stocking stuffers—only ten bucks."

Why not? he'd thought. He knew it was just the thing to cheer Johnny up. In all his anger, he'd forgotten it was there. He relaxed, only slightly. He knew he only wanted to argue, to dump all his frustrations on someone, and he was wise enough to get away from his wife before he started an argument with her. *That's all she needs right now.*

Well, God, you're getting one of David's prayers tonight, he thought silently, and he began to dump all his problems on God. He prayed all the things he'd wanted to say while he was kneeling in his son's room.

Do something about that little bully, Lord. Get him suspended—better yet, get him expelled. Make his family move, make him sick, I don't care—keep him away from my son!

He understood why his son was a target for the bully. Last summer, the bully rode the church bus most Sundays to attend their church, and his wife had been his Sunday school teacher. He picked on the other children, and disrupted the class every week. Most Sundays his wife had to send him out from the class, or the other children would hear nothing of the lesson. Often, he waited on the swings until church was over, and bullied the other kids while they played and their parents talked. One Sunday he started a fight down by the swings, and his wife heard the ruckus when they stepped out from the church. She rushed down to the swings, pulled the bully off another boy, and brought him to the pastor's office. The boy never came back to church. Johnny's father knew the pastor well; he was sure he had only told the bully he would need to treat the other children better, but it was enough embarrassment for the boy to never return. When school started that fall, the bully gave special attention to his son.

"Your church is *stupid,*" the bully had taunted him. "Church is for *girls.* Look at the pretty *girl*; he loves his *mommy's* Sunday school classes." That's how it had started, and it had been going on all year.

His head flashed hot with anger, temporarily warding off the night's chill. When it wore off, he thought about heading home. He looked around him; he'd hardly paid attention to where he was walking.

How did I end up here? he asked himself. He'd walked at least a dozen blocks from his home. He heard a police siren in the distance, and scanned the road for a street sign. Suddenly, he recognized where he was. The one time he'd filled in for his church's bus driver, the bully had been onboard. He was approaching the block the boy lived on.

Good, he thought to himself. *I've had enough of this.* He quickened his pace. He resolved to tell the boy's parents just what he thought of their son. In a momentary lapse of character, he imagined the boy's father spanking him, and relished the thought.

Many of the houses were dark, though it wasn't late. Very few of them had Christmas lights up. He knew the area had been hit especially hard in the recent economy's downturn. Several of the houses had recent foreclosure notices still tacked to their front doors. *Wow*, he thought, *what a horrible time of year to evict someone.* He heard a scream and his eyes darted, looking for its source. A loud voice boomed in return. He jogged around the corner, and saw an unhappy scene played out in a living room window.

Strange lights danced over the snow-capped bushes in the house's front yard, while a commercial shone brightly from a television screen. The house and yard were in worse wear than the emptied foreclosures surrounding it. A man and a woman shouted at each other, in plain view of their front window.

Some people, he thought to himself. He caught himself, stopped the disapproving shake of his head, just in time to see the man reach out and slap the women, hard in the face. He stopped dead in his tracks, unsure what he should do. He had nearly reached their house. While he struggled between calling the police and rushing to the front door, the woman left the room with a muffled sob. The man stormed out the front door, leaving it wide open behind him.

"Where are you going?" he heard the tearful voice from within the house.

"I'm out of whiskey," the man yelled as he slammed his car door. He backed out of the driveway, turned, and slid on the ice as he gunned the engine. Johnny's father jumped into the neighbor's yard just in time, right over the snow-covered sidewalk; the old car hopped the curb onto the sidewalk near where he'd been standing. The driver overcorrected and knocked over the mailbox across the street before finding his way to the right lane.

"Get out of the way, *moron*," he heard from the car as it sped away.

Shaken, he stepped back onto the street and stomped his feet to clear the snow from his socks and pant legs once again. He shivered, thinking of the frigid wind blowing into the still-open front door of the house. He took quick strides toward it, unwilling to leave it open. He prayed he could shut it and slip away without being noticed.

He closed the door gently, and tip-toed back down the driveway. A rustle in a large bush in the yard stole his attention. The shadowy outline of a headless torso nearly made him jump.

"Who's there?" a scared child's voice cried.

"Just a stranger, out on a walk," was all he could muster. The boy's head popped out from the zippered collar of an old coat. He'd been *lying down* inside the bush. He yanked a pair of earphones from his ears and threw them down. "Stupid thing's broken." Then he turned back, his eyes open wide in recognition. "You're no stranger," he shot back. "You're *Johnny's dad.*"

He jerked his head slightly in surprise. If he hadn't been distracted by the argument in the window, he might have guessed this house was the home of Billy, his son's tormentor.

"That's right Billy, I am," he said when he recovered. "What are you doing outside?" he asked. Concern had found its way into his voice; he'd never considered this boy might be a *victim*. Something deep in his heart wrestled over how he perceived this young boy.

"It's *Bill*," the boy replied, forcing his voice gruff. "Are you here to tell on me? You just want to get me in trouble."

"No, son, I don't." He was surprised to find this was true; he didn't want to add to this boy's pain. "Now *what are you doing out here?*"

Billy wiped his nose. In the light from the window, he saw a trace of dried blood where it had trickled from one nostril earlier that evening.

"I left...they were fighting again." He stood and started to unzip his coat. Johnny's dad reached out to stop him, and as he did, he felt his hands—they were shivering.

"Why are you taking your coat off?"

"It's *his*—my mom's boyfriend's. I—I have to put it back before he comes home." Fear shone brightly in his eyes.

"Just wait a minute, Bill; he won't be back right away." There was a weathered terrace beside the bush, and Johnny's father sat down on it. "Why don't you tell me why you're out here?" He took a closer look at the boy's nose, and found his answer.

"I just put on my earphones when they fight. But tonight...well, after I came out here, I guess I fell asleep." Billy's voice cracked, and he looked away, shivering. Johnny's father realized why his head had been tucked down into his coat—he had no hat or hood over his head. He took off his own, and handed it to him.

"Here, put this on, or you'll freeze." Billy paused before reacting. Suspiciously, he pulled it over his head.

"You really aren't going to tell my mom—you know, about Johnny?" he asked. Hesitantly, he sat beside him on the terrace. Billy's hands were shaking.

Johnny's father wavered. His anger over Johnny being bullied was closer to his heart, but Billy's circumstances were so grave, he found he had little anger left toward him.

"Take these," he said, handing him his gloves. "You look a good deal colder than me tonight." Billy quickly put them on, and shoved his hands into his pockets. "You brought up a good point though. Johnny's not having a very fun night either. I won't bother your mom, but maybe *you* can help me." Billy looked away again, not wanting to meet his gaze. "It's Johnny's mom you're mad at, isn't it?"

Billy choked back a sob and nodded quickly. Then he coughed, and cleared his throat. "You going to tell him I'm a crybaby now?"

"No, Billy, I'd never embarrass you like that." He wondered at the change in heart he had for the boy, in only a minute's time. This bully suddenly looked like a whole other person to him. "My wife didn't want to embarrass you either, on that Sunday last summer. She only wanted to protect the kid you were fighting with. He was a couple years younger than you, right?"

"Yeah. I do stupid things like that sometimes."

"We all do, Bill," he said, smiling warmly. "Sometimes when we're hurting, we're tempted to hurt others. It never makes us feel better for long." He paused, wondering what he could possibly say next. "You know what? Johnny was sad when you stopped coming to church. He kind of looked up to you back then."

"He did? I didn't know that."

"Do you think you can work things out with Johnny— you know, find a way to work things out *without fighting?*"

Billy coughed back another sob.

"Yes sir...I can do that."

"I'm very glad to hear it. You know what? It's time you got back inside." A thought flashed through his mind— when he had closed the door to the house, the air rushing out wasn't all that warm. "Do you have heat in there tonight?"

"The heater broke last week."

Alarmed, he reached for the boy's shoulder. "Billy, does your hot water still work?"

"Yeah, it does."

He sighed inwardly. "You need a hot bath before you go to bed. Will you promise me you'll get a really hot bath, and put on all your covers?"

"Promise?" Billy repeated, clearly doubting his concern.

"Yes, I want you to promise. I have something for you if you do." He reached into his jacket pocket and found the MP3 player he'd bought for his son. He dangled it between his fingers.

"*For real?*" Billy asked. "Sure, I promise. I'll take *two* baths," he added, smiling.

"All right then." Johnny's father smiled as he handed it to him, and stood to leave. Billy pulled off his hat and gloves, and held them out.

"Don't forget these."

"That's fine, son, you keep them. It's not a long walk for me," he exaggerated. He could jog back home to stay warm if he needed to. Billy smiled at him, then looked back at the empty driveway before his gaze dropped to the ground. "Hurry up now, it's getting late."

Billy walked back to the front door. He turned back and waved just before going in.

Johnny's dad felt better than he'd felt in weeks. He was beginning to feel prideful for the little talk he had with Billy. *God*, he prayed silently, *what have you done to me? Why do I see him so differently now?* A strange thought formed in his mind.

Do I truly see him differently, or have I merely felt empathy for him for the first time?

In his mind's eye, he saw a younger Billy, and suddenly, he truly *did* see him differently. It was early summer, and Billy looked younger, but also innocent and confused. He was running from his house crying, his mother's boyfriend yelling after him.

"When you come back, you're *really* going *to get it,*" the man shouted.

He winced at the scene he saw in his mind. He saw several more, in rapid succession. First he saw Billy slapped by the same man, for waking him on his day off, then crying while he waited for the church bus minutes later. He saw Billy picking on younger kids hours later, after church. He saw the man taunting Billy that afternoon, for going to church, and he felt Billy's determination ebbing away.

Then, he saw the lessons God wanted Billy to learn every Sunday, instead of the lessons of hate he was learning at home. A great pain grew in him when he understood God's heart for Billy, a powerful love, a great desire to protect him from his mother's boyfriend, to get him out of the house when the man was drunk and abusive to him and his mother. His heartache grew as he saw Billy in Sunday school for the last time. In his mind, he saw through Billy's eyes in the small classroom. He nearly gasped when he saw *himself* teaching the class.

A memory flooded into his mind as the bitter wind bit through his jacket. His wife had grown increasingly frustrated, trying to maintain order in her Sunday school class. The breath flew from his lungs when he remembered his wife, exhausted from dealing with Billy, asking him to fill in for her, to teach the class in her place. He felt like he'd been punched in the gut, and for a quick moment, he couldn't breathe.

God wanted me to teach Billy all the lessons his father never could. To his shame, he remembered feeling *glad* when the boy didn't come back to church. *One less problem*, he'd thought.

More scenes played in his mind—they weren't memories—but instead shadows of a lost past. He saw Billy eating Sunday dinner as a guest in his home, coming to family barbecues, running, laughing, *playing* with his son, instead of passing on the abuse he received at home. *This* is what God wanted for Billy.

I could've helped, but didn't. What excuses did I give my wife for not taking over her class? He couldn't remember, not one of them. In reality, it mattered little; they were as worthless as any excuse is. *Why didn't I listen? I heard the faint call of God when she asked me, but I ignored it.* His throat stabbed with horror as he realized not only Billy, but *his son* was paying for his unwillingness to do what was right. *Oh, God, take this memory from me; don't let me see it any longer.*

Suddenly, he saw his son Johnny in his mind. He looked almost like a small man to him—he seemed older, upright and strong. He looked *mighty.* His father's heart crumbled with pain as he saw Johnny stand up for his mother, even for his church while Billy mocked him at school. Anger toward Billy flashed through him, until the fresh memory of what he'd been shown washed it away. A great pride for his son swelled in him, and pieced his pained heart back together. His son was learning great lessons through his pain, maturing with a strong knowledge of forgiveness, longsuffering, and a great commitment for standing up for what is true and right. It was almost too strong to hold, the dual emotions of heavy grief and pride, to see his son in God's eyes.

When he reached home, his children had gone to bed, and his wife was sitting at the kitchen table. She stood and walked over to him as he hung his jacket and took off his shoes. She leaned into his chest and held him tightly. She pulled back from him suddenly when she felt his ears and face.

"Oh—*your face is like ice,*" she started, "Why didn't you wear your hat?" But he didn't answer right away, and she saw a trace of tears on his cheek. He looked deeply into her eyes and saw she'd also been crying. They embraced in the doorway for a long minute. Her expression relaxed, and she smiled warmly, as if she knew something had changed in his heart. He led her to the kitchen table and sat in the chair beside her own.

"Let me tell you what I saw tonight," he said excitedly, "you'll never believe what happened." His voice nearly cracked, and his gaze dropped to the table. Her Bible and notepad were still there, but the page that had only a single line when he'd left, was filled. Several random words were smeared from wet tears dropped onto the paper. His gaze locked on the single line he'd seen before he stormed out of the house, and he knew she wouldn't find his story difficult to believe at all. He read the line over again, smiling wide.

Ps 68:5-6a: *Take away his anger Lord, let him see Billy* in your eyes.

She followed his gaze, then, reading his face, her expression changed.

"Go talk to your son," she urged him. "He's reading in bed." He nodded, and went right to him, eager to catch him before he fell asleep.

When he opened the door, he saw his son's eyes pop open.

"Did I wake you?" he asked, while he sat on the edge of the bed. His reading lamp was on, and his Bible was open.

"No, Dad, I'm awake." He was in better spirits then when he'd left.

"Son, I wanted to tell you something important. God opened my eyes tonight, and I saw many things about you."

Johnny's eyes dropped to the bed, and his face grew long and uncertain. "God showed me what is in your heart, how *He* sees you. I've never felt more proud." They embraced in a great bear hug, and Johnny's eyes sparkled with joy.

"Was it…about Billy?"

"Yes, it was. I also saw what Billy looks like in God's eyes. I won't burden you with the details, but I need to tell you, God has important things to teach Billy too. He has a very sad home, Johnny. He's in a…dangerous situation."

"I know his mom's boyfriend beats him sometimes," Johnny said quietly.

"Let's pray for him, too. I think the forgiveness you've shown Billy is about to change his life." He had no reason why he should feel this way, but it was such a powerful feeling, he was somehow certain it would come to pass.

They prayed together, then Johnny talked to his father a long while, about Billy, about school, and many other things his father wished he'd known before. He kissed Johnny on the top of the head, and tucked him in.

Later, lying in bed, Johnny's parents held each other tight. They talked about all the things they'd seen and been praying for. Before turning out the light, they prayed together, for their son, and also for Billy.

"Why don't we do this every night?" Johnny's mother asked. "We used to pray together before going to sleep all the time." Johnny's father smiled and nodded. Nothing sounded better to him.

When he rolled over and began to fall asleep, he thought his night was over—but he was very wrong. He tossed and turned fitfully in his sleep, and had a dream so vivid, it seemed more real to him than life. In his dream, he saw himself from across the room, as if he was watching a movie of himself. He pulled the evening newspaper from its plastic sleeve and unfolded it. Fear gripped him when he saw the headline—"Family Dies, Drunk Driving, Exposure, Suicide." He followed the story to its end. The man who'd nearly ran him over had driven off the road just miles from his home. He was pronounced dead at the wreck site when the police found him in the morning. Billy had died of exposure; his mother found him lying in the bushes of their front yard. She took her own life just after she found him.

How could he go back outside? His heart cried out, buried in sudden grief. He cried out to God, *"Why?"* loudly enough to be heard from the street. His scream took on a frightening pitch and stretched out long and twisted. He screamed so loud in his dream, it woke him. He lay still as death, bathed in sweat. He wiped his brow and found his hands were trembling. He began fervently praying, for Billy, for his mother, and for her boyfriend. Though he resolved to drive to Billy's house and check on his family, he fell asleep during his prayers.

When he woke, he bolted upright in bed. *The newspaper,* he recalled in horror. Guilt for falling back asleep washed over him. He would not wait until the paper was delivered. He rushed to get dressed, and woke his wife in his haste.

"Dear," his wife cried out, fear edging into her voice, "what's the matter?"

"I have to go," he said as he rushed out of the room. He called over his shoulder, "I'll call you from my car." On the short drive, his wife barely got any information from him. She began to worry for him as he drove. Unexpectedly, she heard him cry, "Oh God, no!" his voice raising a full octave in pitch, then…silence.

"What happened? *Are you hurt?*" she cried in his ear.

"I'm fine—I'll call you in just a minute," he stammered, as he ended the call and dropped his phone to the seat of his car. There was a state trooper's car in the driveway of Billy's home. *I'm too late,* his mind screamed in desperate fear.

He parked his car across the street and walked slowly to the front door. There was an officer standing outside the door in a heavy coat, sipping coffee.

"Are you family?" the trooper asked.

"No, I'm…uh, an old friend. The boy—Billy—used to come to my church."

The officer's expression changed suddenly. "I guess you've heard about the boyfriend's death," he replied. "Just wait here for a minute."

Without an explanation, he opened the door and quietly stepped into the house, closing the door silently behind him.

What could I have done differently? His mind raced. *Could I have prevented this?* A moment later, the trooper returned.

"You can go in. The boy and his mother could use a friend right now."

"What—they're both inside?" He felt the air pulled from his chest. He was afraid to hope. The trooper's expression flashed with suspicion.

"Look—are you sure you're alright?"

"Yes, I'm fine," he answered the trooper, walking swiftly past him, into the house.

The house was sparsely furnished, though there was a large, flat panel television hanging on the living room wall, and a small dorm-style fridge beside the couch. Inside, Billy's mother was seated at the kitchen table, across from another trooper. Billy was standing behind his mother, holding her tightly. All of them wore heavy coats, and their breath showed in puffs when they spoke. To the surprise of Johnny's father, Billy ran to him and embraced him. He hugged the boy back. His mother looked up from the table, and she smiled weakly in recognition. Johnny's father recognized her too…she had visited their church often with a baby, years ago. He never realized that baby was Billy.

After a minute, Billy awkwardly left him and returned to his mother. "Can he stay?" Billy asked the trooper.

"I'm afraid not, son. We're going to be here a while, making our reports." The officer nodded toward Johnny's father and added," I thought maybe you might want to go to a friend's house until we're done.

Johnny's father quickly pulled out an old business card from his wallet and tore it in half. He wrote his phone number and address on both pieces. He handed one half to Billy's mother, and kept the other in his hand.

"Johnny can spend the day with us," he began, and Billy's mother quickly gave him a small, appreciative nod before she began crying again. "Come to our house when you're finished, we want you to stay for dinner."

"Hurry over, Mom," Billy said. He kissed her on the cheek, then walked back to Johnny's father.

As he walked out of the house, he looked down at the old business card he'd torn in half. He didn't recognize it at first, then he read the lettering on the remaining half.

...& Sons

...Heating Repair

The card showed half the name of a business, and in the lower right corner, their phone number was listed. It was the company that fixed his air conditioning system last summer, Richards and Sons A/C and Heating Repair. He smiled, silently thanking God for the hint, as he entered the number into his cell phone and saved it. As he closed the door, he handed the half-card to the officer waiting outside.

"Please drive her to my house when you're done," he said politely. "Billy will be with us, and...his mother doesn't need to be alone right now." He didn't know how he could confer his request with any more urgency, but the officer was already nodding. The officer stared knowingly into his eyes, and he knew the officer understood.

"Now then," he said to Billy when they were in his car, "we'll get you back to my house, and get something warm to eat. We'll be there soon; I just need to make a phone call on the way."

After he'd called the heating repairman, Billy looked worried.

"I don't think my mom can pay to fix the heater," he said anxiously.

"Don't worry," Johnny's father answered with a smile, "It's all taken care of." He knew the bonus he was expecting from work wouldn't be spent as he'd planned. He looked back to Billy, but found his expression hadn't changed.

"What's worrying you, Billy?"

"Well," he began sheepishly, "I haven't been...very nice to Johnny. Do you think he'll forgive me?"

"I bet he will. Maybe you should ask him when he wakes up. I think he'll be a true friend to you—if you treat him like one." He pulled into his driveway and turned off the engine. Still, Billy didn't seem relieved—if anything, he looked frightened.

"Do you think..." he stopped. Johnny's father waited patiently. Billy didn't look ready to leave the car; in fact, he was nearly in tears. "I've been asking Him to...but—do you think *God* will forgive me?

"In God's eyes," Johnny's father answered with a confident smile, "He already has."

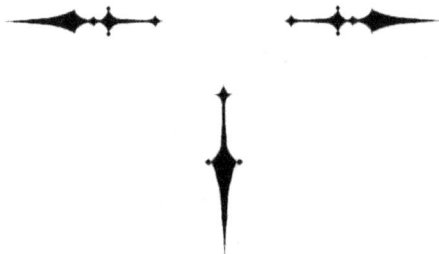

When God Whispers Loudly

He was late, rushing to his daughter's piano recital from a job that took all his strength to leave while it was still daylight. Driving *just a little over* should get him to the recital before his daughter finished playing.

Earlier the same day, he found he'd been passed over for a promotion. Worse yet, it had been given to a man ten years his junior. His new boss was the man in his office he least respected, and in his mind, least deserved the job. As if it were related, he felt disappointed his commitment to his family hadn't affected his children the way he'd hoped. In reality, he was angry it cost him his dream job.

The winding road on his route led him past an empty field before a sharp turn and a sign which read *CAUTION*.

"Why, God?" he prayed, his brow set firm. He thought of his wife's email, reminding him to leave work early for yet another of his children's activities. "Why do I have to sacrifice everything, and she only asks for *more?*" He knew it was reactionary and selfish, but for the moment he allowed his anger to lead him just the same.

As he sped around the corner, he prayed he wouldn't have to go to work the next day and see his new boss—*the weasel*—sitting in the office *he* deserved. The road was wet and he crept into the opposing lane—and as his did, he faced an oncoming lumber truck which had also crossed the center line.

As he swerved he prayed, "I didn't mean it—*save me.*" Fleeting relief came as he narrowly missed the truck, then slid off the road, out of control. Still far over the speed limit, his car struck a gnarled, bent oak and turned over. Once— twice—it rolled, then finally came to rest on its roof, leaving him dangling from his seatbelt.

He woke unable to move and surrounded in chaos. It took him a moment to realize he was in a hospital. He felt his consciousness slipping, and fought in vain to keep it.

He heard voices as his eyelids closed, "…prepped for surgery", and "Get him to the OR…" He heard his wife crying not far off, and for a moment he thought he would fight his way back to consciousness—but he was wrong.

He next woke in familiar surroundings. He was lying in the guest bed of his own home, only it was somehow different. His wife stood at the foot of the twin bed where he laid, while a small group of young adults crowded around him. His wife was smiling, tears rolling down her face. The curious group of strangers stared at him anxiously, some smiling, some crying. Others stood still with their eyes closed peacefully.

"…*he's waking,*" one of the strangers in his room whispered.

"God," he prayed silently, suddenly panic stricken, "please don't let me be paralyzed."

His mind reasoned, *it's a group from church, come to pray for me.* It would explain the young men and women standing over him in bed—though he strained to recognize them. To his relief, he was able to sit up, though it required more effort than he expected.

His wife dropped to his bedside and threw her arms around him. He cradled her head on his shoulder, but her embrace felt unfamiliar. Her shape didn't conform to his own as his muscle memory expected. His own body seemed unfamiliar, as if he'd instantly lost weight. His joints were stiff, and they ached when he moved. He looked around the room wondering who the young men and women were, intruding upon such a private moment. He noted how familiar the eldest young lady was; she looked like a younger version of his wife. Only then did his mind register what his wife was saying as she wept on his shoulder.

"You're back, you're finally awake—I *knew* you'd come back to us."

Confused, he pulled back from her embrace and looked hard into her face. Her hair was grayed, and the lines on her face were deeper, further reaching.

"How long?" he asked, his voice an uncertain grumble. His wife shook her head, not wanting to answer at first.

"*Fifteen years,*" she whispered tearfully.

Over the next day he didn't have a single moment alone. He spent every precious minute with his wife, his children and their spouses. He found it bittersweet, coming to know his children again.

His daughter was married to a fine man, unashamed of his commitment to Christ. They had a child of their own, his first grandchild. They had begun the next cycle in the wonderful gift of life God gives so freely. He found his daughter just as strong in her commitment to God, alive and vibrant.

"But you seemed so *angry*," the father said at one point. "I was so afraid you wouldn't listen to God; you might ignore His still, small voice."

"I did, Daddy—I ignored it for a long time," she replied. "But He showed me. He used *you* to show me. All the times you were patient with me…all the times you waited up for me, the times you prayed over me as a little girl…the times I heard you praying under your breath when you thought no one was near. They all pointed me to Him. So many times, Daddy…" and she told him of all the little ways he'd shown her God's love. He began to feel proud of the example he'd been to her. Proud, that is, until she began to list things he couldn't remember. Then she listed things he *knew* he hadn't done.

Who is she remembering? he wondered. *How could she confuse someone else with her own father?* His expression grew more concerned until his daughter noticed.

"What's wrong?" she asked. But it was too perfect a day, too wonderful a time to dispute her.

"It's nothing. My mind must be tired—not used to being awake, I guess."

And so it went with his sons. When they each told how they'd lived out their childhood, each pointed to memories of significant choices in their lives; of steps in their spiritual maturity. They each mentioned a talk he'd given or lesson he'd taught they later realized had influenced them. Just as with his daughter, some he'd remembered, and others he didn't. His youngest son mentioned a private talk he was sure he hadn't given to him; it was a talk he'd given his older children when they reached an age he'd missed in his youngest child's life.

Who gave my youngest boy this speech while I was trapped in a coma? he wondered. *He must have heard his older brothers tell the story so often, he felt like he'd heard it first hand*, the father thought.

Gradually a great wave of accomplishment, a feeling of unashamed *success* washed over him as he spoke with his children and he saw firsthand how each one of them had begun their adult lives. He shared this thought with his wife the next morning as they sat together in their backyard. His sons had talked with him straight through the night.

"What did you expect?" asked his wife, so familiar to him, yet eerily different in her appearance. "Did you think they would abandon God, they would live out their lives as lost sheep?"

"Of course not," he answered. "I guess I was only *hopeful* they would follow Him so closely. After all, it's a choice each of them must make for themselves."

She gave him a look of shared knowledge. Without looking for it, he realized the deep wisdom in her eyes. She had matured for 15 years while he slept, and he now felt somehow lesser to her. He wondered at the years of wise choices sparkling in her eyes.

"I love you so much," she said, and a thought struck him hard in the chest.

Those aren't idle words. She'd brought him back from the hospital after months of unresponsiveness. She'd moved him back into their home and cared for him fifteen long years. She'd cleaned him; she'd rolled him over and treated his bedsores. She'd fed him for a *decade and a half* as he lay there, unresponsive as death.

What commitment, he thought, but directly afterward, he knew she could have done nothing less—not from obligation, but from her strong character and devotion he knew so well. Suddenly, he knew she'd been just as committed to him and their children in all the years before his coma. Somehow he'd neglected to recognize her powerful and steadfast love; a love strong enough to carry his family through the long years he laid sleeping.

She was far more committed than I. He saw the love in her eyes, the endurance she'd shown as a single mother raising their family while he'd slept.

"How were you all waiting in my room when I woke?" he asked through watery eyes.

"*Your toes*," she laughed. "You started wiggling your toes yesterday morning. When I had the doctor stop by, he found your brainwave patterns were beginning to change. The kids came home to be here just in case. We took turns with you all yesterday, so we could all be with you, if you woke. When you began to stir, we all rushed in. The next thing we knew you were *awake*."

After sitting alone with his wife for most of the morning, his children and their spouses took turns spending more time with him. They kept him awake as long as they could, to the point when he could hide his weariness no longer.

"*Please, let me sleep*. We have the rest of our lives to catch up," he told his eldest son at one point.

"No, Daddy. Let me spend a little more time with you," he replied, "I've waited so long to talk with you again."

The irony of the tall, strong man before him calling him *Daddy* was more than enough to dissuade him. Eventually, even getting to know his grown children couldn't keep his eyelids from falling. As if being sleep's prisoner for fifteen years wasn't enough, he began to succumb to its call. His eldest son lifted him from the bench in the yard—as easily as if he were a feather—and carried him to his bed. His wife and children gathered around him once again as it became obvious he would soon be asleep. They had talked and sat with him for an entire day and night, keeping him awake through the following morning.

"We love you so much Daddy," his daughter said, and all echoed their affection for him, just as tearfully as when he first awoke.

"I'll be awake in a few hours," he lied, sadly aware of the warning he'd overheard the doctor giving his family only hours ago, thinking he was out of earshot.

"*He may return to normal after today,*" *his doctor had said, after performing a few tests. "But I fear it's not likely. His brainwaves aren't normal—they're still too close to those we find in a comatose patient. I don't understand how he's awake and responsive with such minimal brainwave activity.*"

"*It's a miracle,*" *said his wife, and the doctor agreed.*

"*Yes, but even miracles don't last forever. I'm afraid when he next falls asleep, he's not likely to wake again. I'm so very sorry.*"

When he could fight it no longer, he simply closed his teary eyes. As he did, he heard his grown children and wife quietly mourn losing him once again. And yet—sleep didn't come as he expected. He wasn't able to open his eyes or feel his body, but he was able to hear. He listened as his children and wife each came near and whispered to him, as he lay still as death.

He wondered, "Is this what a coma feels like—did I somehow forget? Will I be trapped forever, able only to hear—wishing every day for death?"

As alarming as the thought was, he didn't feel distressed; in fact, an unexpected peace seemed to envelope him. He realized all he'd wanted out of life had come to pass. He'd seen his children grown, each so familiar with the joy of serving Christ, each raised by the loving hand of his wife and his God, graceful through all. He saw his wife, and knew her needs—physical, spiritual and emotional—had been met by God, and also by the support of their grown children.

"I can die now," he thought, "I am complete". Immediately he was bombarded by the memory of his thoughts from the night of his accident—and he knew how foolish he'd been.

"How does a promotion compare with this: to see my children grown and successful: committed to God and enjoying the peace only He can bring—to see my wife, cared for and surrounded by them, a loving family knit so close together? If I'd been promoted, it could in no way have added to this great treasure."

Inwardly, he wept for how he'd taken so much in his life for granted. He understood how he'd often abandoned this peace for some pathetic imitation he'd fleetingly desired. He saw how he frequently he'd traded God's treasures for pale substitutions, mere shadows of what he truly wanted. The perspective was unbearable to him.

"How could I have missed it?" he asked himself, gradually sick with the bitter taste of regret in his mouth. "How could I have been so blind?" He begged God to grant him one last request. "Tell them Lord—show them what I now see. Don't let this revelation go to waste." Then, amazingly, he heard God reply. At first he wondered, "Am I dying?" Quickly, he shoved the thought aside to listen to the voice in his mind's ear.

"Yes, I will tell them. I will call them, and I will tell them this same message I've been telling you for so long...this message you chose not to hear. Why did you ignore me, dear child? I told you every day, and showed you in a thousand ways, but you were too busy to listen. How loudly must I whisper before you hear Me?"

He wept bitterly to hear such revealing truth.

"I told you so often..." he heard God again, *"but don't be bitter now. Let go your regret..."*

It was too much to take in at once. The words rung all too loudly in his mind as he lay there, motionless. And as amazingly as falling asleep and not waking for fifteen years, he awoke that night without falling asleep at all.

"...relax...relax..." he thought he heard God's voice telling him. Then louder, more brashly, "You have to *lie back* and *relax.*"

He tried again to sit up, and a nurse far too powerful for her small frame leaned her forearm against his shoulder. "*Lie down,*" she continued shouting, clearly unconcerned with offending him. "Your family is *fine.* Your wife is waiting in the next room."

"What—" he stammered, "what's happening?"

"I told you. You've been in a car accident, and you've had emergency surgery. The drugs are still wearing off. You're not going to remember any of this, so *lie back and relax.*"

But he *did* remember; he remembered *everything.*

"What kind of accident?" he asked, "Did I hit a tree? Was I in a coma?"

"A coma? You haven't had time for that. Now lay still and *relax,* or you'll pull your stitches. Your wife will meet you in recovery soon enough—she got here almost as soon as the ambulance. I told her you're going to be fine, but she's worried just the same," the nurse said, shaking her head.

"No coma? The accident...*was today?*"

"The ambulance arrived just a few hours ago," replied the nurse, pressing even harder into his shoulder.

"Thank you, Lord," he whispered quietly, eyes closing. At last he made sense of the words his children in his dream had remembered, the words he'd spoken but couldn't recall.

They're instructions, not memories—God sent me instructions *in my dream.* Then, unexpectedly, other words rang again in his ears—the words God had whispered so loudly to him that day—so loudly it nearly killed him.

"I told you every day, and showed you in a thousand ways... How loudly must I whisper before you hear Me?"

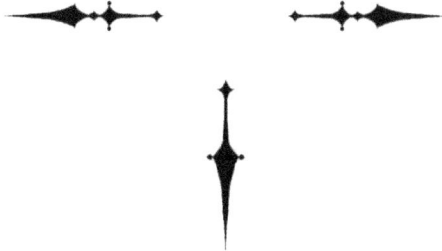

Chris M. Hibbard

God's Worn Out Servants

©2013 Tattie Maggard
Terreldor.com

I quit teaching Sunday school the day my best friend nearly killed her eight-month-old son. My pastor said I just needed time to recover, that the kingdom needed workers like me, but I knew then I would quit forever.

It had been unseasonably cool that April. It was one of those years when the groundhog had gotten it all wrong, and it seemed like winter would never end.

I was in my early thirties and too busy to realize how chaotically I was living. I remember thinking being a stay at home mom would be easy. I expected to have plenty of time to clean, do laundry, run errands, and cook, with time left over to enjoy afternoon tea with my sister now and then. As my children came, first Evan, then Jessica, and unexpectedly Sarah, my life seemed to spin out of control.

Richard was working long hours to make ends meet, and I was trying to pick up the slack at home. I already did all of the housework, but soon found myself doing the outside chores as well. I took out the garbage, mowed the lawn, and trimmed the hedges. I took the vehicles in for oil changes and inspections, and plunged every clogged toilet. Then there was all the taxiing: doctor appointments, soccer practice, ballet lessons, and after-school activities. I was the world's busiest supermom, and that was only my weekdays.

On weekends, I served as church secretary and Sunday school teacher for first through fourth graders. Our church was few in number, and most weren't members. Most of the volunteer work fell to my best friend, Kallie, and me. The rest were unwilling or unreliable. We cleaned the church once a week, cooked most of the food for monthly pot-luck dinners, and were responsible for any other special occasions that came up. It was a lot of work, but I considered it an offering to God. After all, who would do it if not us? We were wearing ourselves thin and starting to dread church altogether. It was what God wanted us to do, I was sure, though I felt no closer to Him doing it.

"Pastor had better quit giving those kids gum before church, or he's going to have to start scraping it off the seats himself," Kallie complained as we were cleaning the sanctuary one day. I got to know Kallie pretty well from the time we spent serving together. Over time, our cleaning sessions turned into gripe sessions. We vented about our kids, our husbands, and everything in between. It wasn't as if we could complain to anyone else, and letting off a little steam was therapeutic for us both. Some people watch TV, others have a glass of wine, but Kallie and I had each other.

Kallie held down a full time job, was finishing a college degree, and did most of the same work I did at church. She was the only friend I had who wasn't a stay-at-home mom, probably because she never made me feel badly about it. I was far busier than I'd been before I quit my job. I felt like I understood why so many women chose to work outside of the home. Sometimes the jealousy worked both ways, but I'd never let that show to any of my friends. I was "living the dream."

"You know, I dread coming here tomorrow," Kallie said with a painful expression. "It's awful, I know, but just once I wish I could rest on Sunday instead of feeling like I'm going to work." She wound up the vacuum cord onto its hooks. Her dark pony tail swayed as she worked, and the cord swung back and forth.

"I know it. I can't remember the last time I got to just sit and listen to a sermon or a Sunday school class. It's probably a good thing, though. If I sit still more than a few minutes I'll fall asleep."

I gathered the songbooks from each pew, and placed them neatly inside the holder on each of the seat's backs.

"Still staying up late with Evan?" she asked.

"Yeah. With his practice running late and Sarah's ballet lessons, it's dark before we can even get a start on his schoolwork. If he doesn't get his grades up he won't be able to play ball. Honestly, I'm tempted to let it go; at least that would be one less appointment I have to keep up with." I threw my hands in the air in surrender then plopped onto the red-cushioned pew.

Kallie laughed. "Did you play ball when you were young?"

"No way. My mother didn't have time to take us anywhere."

"And you turned out okay…right?" Kallie wheeled the vacuum out the side door of the sanctuary. I could hear the wheels reach the hardwood floor then roll down the hall and into the broom closet in the back. When I heard her footsteps near the door, I continued.

"I know… I just want to be a good parent."

Kallie gave me the look that said, *come on.*

"I need to drop a few activities, but I haven't figured out which ones yet. With college, a full time job, and kids, how do you do it? You're the superwoman around here."

"I don't know. Sometimes I feel like I'm just a zombie, you know? I feel like I'm just going through the motions." She stopped and looked around the now-clean sanctuary. "I really don't have time for *this* but I'd feel guilty not to help. Pastor doesn't have any help around here but us."

"Do you know what Carol asked me last Sunday?" Carol was our church's oldest and most contrary member.

"She asked you where in the Bible you'd been studying," Kallie said flatly.

"How'd you know?" I asked.

"She's been asking everyone that. It was only a matter of time until she got to you."

"What did *you* say?" I turned around with my knee in the seat to face my friend.

"I told her I was too busy to study anything other than my college books right now."

"That was...honest. What'd she say?" Carol had a way of being very direct with people.

"She said she'd been asking everyone in the church that question and so far only pastor, and apparently herself, study the bible on a regular basis outside of church. She said that was a shame."

"I would...if I had the time." I tried once again to decide if I was doing something wrong. "It's ironic, you know. I don't have time to study the Bible because I'm too busy working at church."

"It's crazy. We're too busy for Jesus. There's something seriously wrong about that, but for the life of me I don't know how to fix it."

She chuckled half-heartedly, but I could tell her thoughts made her feel the same way they did me: confused. How could we be working so hard trying to do everything right, but still be wrong?

"I've got to get out of here. Jason has to leave in a bit and our usual sitter just quit. See you later, Melanie."

"Take care, Kallie," I said as she hurried out the double doors in the back of the sanctuary. With the cleaning done, I turned out the lights and locked up, but my mind was still full of clutter.

My worries plagued me throughout the week. I began to see all the unnecessary things I was doing—all the busy work that was my own choosing. It was time to cut something out, but what? How could I tell Evan he couldn't play ball, or tell Jessica she had to quit ballet? What would Sarah want to do in a few years? I was already teaching the children to pick up after themselves, and we ate too much fast food for lack of time. How could I make more time for God and would there ever be any time left for me?

"What about question twenty-two?" I asked Evan at the kitchen table late that evening.

"It's extra credit. I don't have to do it."

"If it's extra credit, it could help you get your math grade up."

"But Mom, I'm so tired. Can't I just go to bed?" His brown eyes pleaded with mine.

"Evan." I paused. Could he be looking for a way out as well? The thought had never crossed my mind before. "What would you think about giving up some of your extracurricular activities? Then you could sleep longer."

His face fell. "Fine. I'll do it. Give me the book." He held his hand out.

"Don't you get tired of all the running?" I asked.

"I said I'll do it, okay?"

I gave him the book and watched him meticulously work out the math problem.

"Is the answer seventy-eight?" he asked at last. I punched in the numbers in the calculator and nodded my head.

"Goodnight, Mom," he said, then quickly disappeared down the hallway. Playing ball was what he wanted. He was even willing to do extra credit math problems and lose sleep to do it. I couldn't cut that out.

The next morning I woke up early and made pancakes—not just any pancakes, but chocolate for Evan, strawberry for Jessica and Richard, and blueberry pancakes for Sarah and myself. I even poured them into heart shapes like I used to do, back when I *liked* cooking for my family. Jessica was the first to the table.

"I made your favorite breakfast." I set her plate on the table just as she sat down. Her sleepy-eyed stare was gone the second she laid eyes on her food.

"Strawberry?" she asked.

"You bet."

She happily ate her breakfast as I watched her. She looked different. She was getting taller, thinner; I noticed more freckles on her cheeks. My little girl was growing up. Was I missing it? Would she be college-bound the next time I stopped to think about it? I glanced down the hall.

"Honey, let me ask you something. Are you happy?"

She looked at me quizzically. "Yeah. Aren't you?"

"Yes, sweetie, I'm happy. I was just wondering if you were." Was I really happy? Could I trust her to tell the truth? She nodded her head, still obviously thinking about where this was leading.

"I mean, I wish we could spend more time together— doing girl stuff."

"Like going roller skating?" she asked.

I laughed. "Yeah, like roller skating." The thought of myself on skates made me laugh again. I used to love to roller skate. What was so funny about it?

I'd trade weekly dance lessons for an occasional skate trip.

"Too bad we don't have much time for stuff like that," I said. "If we didn't go to dance, maybe we'd have time."

"Not go to dance?" Her face twisted until I was afraid I'd see tears.

"Oh, no, honey, you can keep going to dance class. Maybe we can find time to go skating sometime, too." I patted her on the back and hoped she'd calm down before Richard walked in the kitchen. He worked overtime to make sure she could continue her lessons. He'd be angry if he thought I was trying to trick her into giving them up. Dance was definitely staying on the schedule, but what was left?

Days went by and every effort to carve out some "free" time was met with resistance on every side, and I couldn't bear to inconvenience anyone. I needed to learn to say no to anything new, and hope some activities would soon end. I daydreamed about what I'd do with a few minutes to myself. I'd love to take a hot bath. Not just a quick shower, but a long, relaxing soak in the tub. Maybe I'd write a letter to my favorite aunt. I hadn't sent her any pictures of the kids in years. How did life get so complicated? Why did I feel like I had to schedule time to use the bathroom? I tried everything to slow down, but nothing was working. I was convinced this was simply the way things were supposed to be. After all, the woman of virtuous character in Proverbs 31 was busy all the time too, wasn't she?

"Melanie," Kallie said to me, the next time we were cleaning together, "would you mind picking up Gracie and taking her to the church fundraiser this afternoon?"

"Sure, but aren't you coming?" Panic was setting in. I couldn't manage this event without her.

"Yes, I'm coming, but I've got a bunch of errands to do, and I have to take Seth to his check-up then get him back to his daddy before the fundraiser starts."

"Did you tell him there wouldn't be any preaching?" I asked. "It's just a fundraiser."

"I know. I told him but he's still not willing to come. He says *church people* are stuffy. He said he'd watch Seth though, so I could help out."

"He'll come around in time."

"I hope so. All right then, I'll have Gracie ready, and you can just swing by and pick her up on your way. Jason will be home. I'll tell him to expect you."

I pulled into Kallie's house, and Gracie ran out the door. I stepped out of the minivan when Jason appeared in the doorway.

"Hi Melanie," he called. "How's your family?"

"We're great. Richard is meeting us at the church later. You should come and visit."

"Oh, I'm kind of busy here, fixing the back porch steps. Maybe another time."

"Sure." I nodded and helped Gracie into the back seat. When I turned around Jason had disappeared. I drove back wondering how the church could reach a person like Jason. Kallie was raised in church, but what about those who weren't—how could we get them interested? We needed an outreach program of some sort.

Suddenly bells were ringing in my head. "*No.* I don't need any new projects," I thought. I turned the radio to the local Christian station and drove on to the church. We were the first to arrive.

I unlocked the doors and instructed the children on what to do. My two oldest children would help while Gracie followed Sarah around, to keep them both out of trouble.

It took an hour of decorating before anyone else showed up. Pastor came in to say *hello*, then went quickly to his study. He was a busy man and it was hard for either of us to find time to talk. As I passed by the door to his study I saw through a crack in the door, he was kneeling on the floor, praying. I wondered why he wasn't helping with the fundraiser. With so many things to do, he just stopped to pray. Was it possible to just *make* time?

The church was soon full of people. Kallie arrived a few minutes after we started, but she got right to work and everything was going smoothly. Things were starting to settle down a bit, but I was feeling uneasy. I'd nearly decided there was no hope for my schedule, but seeing pastor on his knees had changed my mind again. Conviction washed over me. I'd been wrong, and it was time to fix things—time to *make* time. Not *me-time*, but time to let God restore me. How long had it been since I'd really prayed? I didn't mean the usual goodnight prayer or the "please let us have a safe trip" prayer, but real, authentic communion.

"I'm going to step out a minute," I told Kallie, my stomach in a knot.

"Is everything okay?" she asked.

"Yeah, I just need some air."

She nodded but I don't think she really understood. We didn't take breaks, not even when they were offered to us. We certainly would never step out in the middle of a busy church function.

I found Richard on my way out, and told him I was going to step out for a minute. He said he'd go check on Gracie and Sarah. The uneasiness I was feeling was mounting. When I reached the door, I was nearly suffocating. I had to get out, into the sunshine, into the fresh air, into Jesus' arms.

The warm air was refreshing after leaving the air-conditioned church, but soon the humidity was too much. I found myself feeling uneasy, and it wasn't just the weather. I kept walking through the parking lot, crowded with empty cars. I walked on, unsure where I should stop. I wanted to pray, but I felt drawn from the church. My pace quickened.

"God, help me. *Lead me.*" My heart was in a panic when I reached the end of the parking lot. What was I searching for? I turned to my right, and at the end of a long line of cars, a white car stood out. It was parked awkwardly in the grass. We ran out of parking spaces some time ago, and people had begun parking wherever they could fit—*a sign of a successful church event,* I thought.

I was drawn to that car, and suddenly, I found myself running toward it. I didn't know why I felt so strongly, but I was convinced it was urgent. I was still searching for the words to tell God how wrong I'd been, how it was my fault I'd been too busy for Him. I wanted to stop and make amends with Him, but something pressed me further.

I reached the car out of breath. It was Kallie's. I looked around, but saw no one. The urgency I'd felt so strongly was spent. I rested my head on the back window, ready to pour my heart out to God, but as my eyes began to close I saw something out of place: a perfect baby boy asleep in his car-seat in the back. It was Seth.

His mother, Kallie, was inside and Seth was supposed to be with Jason. I remembered seeing Jason just hours before, and him telling me about fixing the porch steps. Kallie forgot to drop him off! I pulled the handle, but no luck. I tried the front passenger door but it was locked too. I ran around the car but both of the driver-side doors were locked as well. I screamed out for help but I doubted anyone would hear. I searched the ditch frantically and found a fist-sized rock.

"God help him," I whispered desperately, as I plunged the rock through the driver-side window, cutting my hand on the broken glass. I hit the unlock-button and opened the back door. I shook the blood from my hand and quickly wiped it on my blouse. I undid the car-seat belts and took the baby in my arms afraid to know if he were alive or dead. I couldn't remember any CPR. I wasn't even sure if that's what he needed. I did the only thing I knew to do; I ran. I put Seth on my shoulder and held him there with both hands while I ran as hard and as fast as I could, back into the church. I remember yelling something as I reached the doors, but I don't remember what it was. Kallie took the baby from me in surprise. Her face held onto disbelief.

"What?" she called out when she saw the blood on my shirt.

"I found him in the car," I cried.

A tall man stepped up to Kallie and said, "Give him to me." Reluctantly, she handed him over. He laid the baby down on the floor and listened to his chest and mouth. I fought tears back to keep from making any noise.

The next thing I recall, I was sitting on the floor. Richard was at my side asking me if I was okay. I looked down at my shirt, covered with my blood. I wondered how bad my hand had been cut.

"Did you call an ambulance?" I asked Richard, thinking of the baby.

"They're on their way. Are you all right? What happened to you?"

"Kallie's little baby..." was all I could eek out. I closed my eyes and prayed with an urgency that pained my heart. I prayed *hard*. I knew Kallie was praying too. We had been too busy for Jesus. Would He be too busy for us?

I heard the man say the baby was breathing steadily, and Richard escorted me into the restroom to wash up. The ambulance arrived a few minutes later, and we watched them load the precious bundle into the back. I didn't know what would happen to Kallie or her baby. Would he live? Would Child Services take him away? Everyone was whispering, no doubt forming their own opinions of who was to blame. I told pastor I wouldn't be teaching Sunday school anymore on the way out.

I'm sure there were all kinds of speculations why Kallie left Seth in the car alone for hours. I was thankful once again the weather was cooler than usual; I'd seen the temperature reach close to one hundred degrees that time of year. I knew why it happened. She was too busy. Pastor said the kingdom needed workers, but I couldn't believe God would approve of us being busy the way we were.

I knew it could have just as easily have happened to me; I could've put my children in danger because my mind was elsewhere. I was too busy to study the Bible, too busy to pray, too busy to stop and invite someone to church. If we didn't have time for God, and we forgot about our families when they needed us the most, what good were we?

I couldn't remember the last time I really put together a good Sunday school lesson. I didn't know who would teach the class, but I knew my heart wasn't in it anymore. I prayed for God to send someone else. I had tried many things to free myself from the burden of a too-tight schedule, but never once thought to pray about it. I had to believe God would help me fix it.

I cried all the way to the hospital. We left the kids with the pastor and his wife, and Richard drove. While my hand hurt, all my thoughts were on baby Seth, and the guilt and shame Kallie would feel if he didn't live. How do you forget your own child? Then I felt a slice of that same guilt and shame myself. I remembered how easily it could have been me. I remembered instances when I'd had face-to-face conversations with people I didn't even remember because I was so tired—and with what, ball practice, or dance? I remembered a time when I'd driven the kids to school, then got home and realized Sarah's car-seat wasn't even fastened to the car. I was too busy to realize; I'd forgotten to check.

I sat quietly while the doctor put seven stitches in my right hand. It was so swollen I couldn't close my fingers and I wondered how the stitches could still fit when the swelling subsided. When the doctor and his nurse left the room I began crying again. I felt Richard's hand on my back and heard him sigh heavily. He never knew what to say in emotional situations.

"It could've been us, Richard," I whispered.

"What do you mean? You'd never leave our kids in the car."

"It was an accident. She didn't mean to do it. She was too busy—just like me."

"What do you mean, too busy?"

"I'm running from daylight till dark every day of the week. I'm not even allowed to get sick. It's too much, Richard. Something bad is going to happen if I don't slow down. This is my wake-up call."

He could tell by the look on my face I was serious. I reserved that look for special occasions.

"Okay, we'll figure something out," he said and helped me off the examination table.

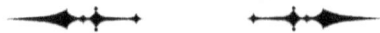

It's been a few years now, and Seth is doing well. Kallie lost him for a while. There was an investigation, but she got him back soon after. She and Jason had to move. There was too much talk, and not enough understanding.

Richard helped me arrange a carpool for Evan's practices and he took on the yard work again. I don't teach Sunday school anymore, but I formed a women's Bible study group in my home that meets every week.

We take turns watching the younger kids so everyone can have a chance to participate. It's helped me to form new relationships and because it's held outside the church, it's become a funnel to bring new visitors to church. They come to my home and meet with other women who love to chat, and drink sweet tea, and read the Bible together. When they grow comfortable with the group they come to church with us. There are lots of people to help out now, and I don't miss teaching the kids a bit. This is where I belong because this is where God has led me. I never would have known that if I hadn't picked up the Bible and just flat out asked Him. Now I make time to read God's word and talk with Him, and it's my goal to lead others to the same.

In the end what will it matter how many church services we attended, or how many church offices we held? Will we be graded on how much money we gave at the church fund raiser? Or will He say, you were very busy but why didn't you make time for me? This is what I remind myself, when deciding what I give my time to. After all, time is the most valuable gift we can give.

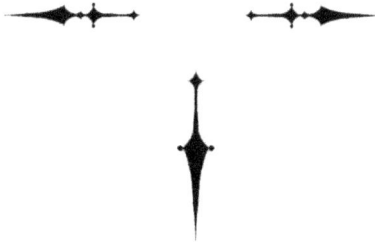

Chris M. Hibbard

Tattie Maggard is a stay at home wife and mother. She runs a popular blog for daily free and cheap kindle books, www.ChristianBookFinds.com. She lives in rural Missouri where the chickens and black bears play in the yard. You can visit her website at http://www.TattieMaggard.com

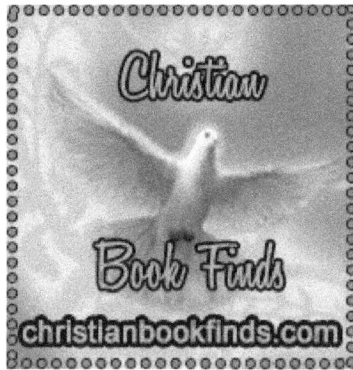

Chris M. Hibbard

To receive release notifications for new books by Chris M. Hibbard, email publishing@Terreldor.com with "notification" in Subject line.

Explore an exciting new world in Chris M. Hibbard's new series:
Adventures in Terreldor

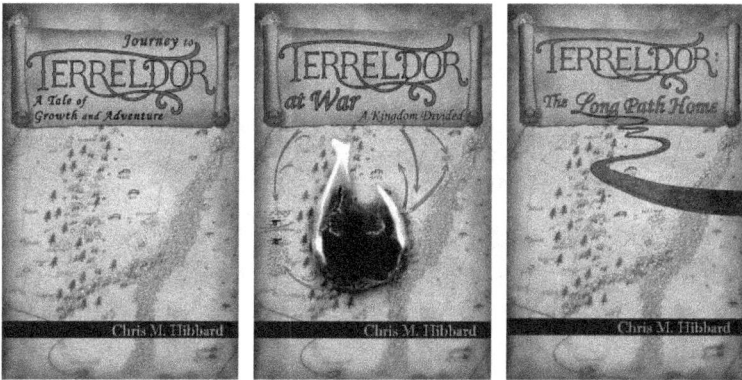

Journey to Terreldor, Terreldor at War
Terreldor: The Long Path Home

availability and details at http://Terreldor.com

Join Mark and his brother as they find themselves in a strange world filled with impossibility and adventure. Faced with tragedy and trial, Mark is forced to draw upon strengths and develop skills he never expected himself capable of. The brothers are taken in by mentors who claim to hold the secrets of true wisdom and maturity. In their endeavors, they learn the most difficult lessons in life are often found on the path home.

Begin the adventure in Journey to Terreldor, then follow these brothers as they are cast into peril in Terreldor at War. Discover the culmination of their odyssey in The Long Path Home. Embark today at Terreldor.com.

Chris M. Hibbard was born in the suburbs of New Jersey, the second of three brothers. His family soon moved to Alaska, where he grew up scrambling over the mountains and beaches of a remote village wedged between thickly wooded peaks and deep fjords. His childhood shaped in him an early love for family and of the outdoors, and inspired such hobbies as wildlife photography, tree grafting, and hiking.

His first novel began as a collection of stories he invented to entertain his children. He, his wife and four children make their home in the Piney Woods of Texas.

Excerpts from C. M. Hibbard's online reviews on iTunes, Kindle, Nook, & Smashwords

"[Hibbard] takes the reader on a thrilling ride…a journey of suspense and adventure." -*Susan Mahoney*

"An original idea and thought-provoking story." -*J. D. Howard*

"A gripping read." -*Sandra Hicks*

"Amazing insight." -*Parul, Amazon user*

"Interesting story with unexpected turns…beautifully written." -*Nook user*

"I would love to see more books by Hibbard." -*Maya, Amazon user*

"So much meaning it leaves you asking what's important in life." -*DebbieS, Amazon user*

"A must read."-*Larry B. Gray* "Amazing!"-*Odetta, Amazon user*

"Leaves you wanting more!" -*Diskson Magombedze*

"Excellent, meaningful book." -*MinisterAsh, iTunes user*

Chris M. Hibbard

A Word on the Typesetting

I had *God's Breaking Heart* set in 12 point Garamond and printed on cream paper—both deliberate choices with the reader and environment in mind. By far, the easier of the two choices was the paper.

The most hazardous chemicals used in the manufacture of paper are the chlorine compounds used in the process of bleaching it white. Cream paper is not only easier on the eyes with its utter lack of glare, it's easier on the environment.

Garamond is considered among the most legible of all typefaces, but it is also heralded as one of the most *green* of the major fonts in terms of ink usage. With such a highly readable font, a 12 point typesetting is effortless to read.

A Brief History of the Garamond Type

The name Garamond describes a collection of humanist serifed typefaces named after the letterpress punch-cutter Claude Garamond (1480–1561), though it is clearly a misattribution. Sixty years after Garamond died, Jean Jannon issued a typeset in France with several similarities to C. Garamond's, though it was unquestionably a new work with undeniable intrinsic value. It is this typeset today's Garamond fonts most resemble.

The French government raided Jannon's office and stole his new typefaces, which were then forgotten for two full decades. When they were next uncovered, they were chosen by the Royal Printing Office as their standard type. Eventually this office evolved into the French National Printing Office, which officially adopted Jannon's type in 1825, erroneously crediting it to Garamond.

New Garamond fonts have poured in throughout the

1900s, predominantly based on the original work by Jannon—even the so-called Garamond-revival fonts. Typographical scholar and journalist Beatrice Warde famously corrected the misnomer in 1925, but by then, the nomenclature had already become permanent.

An inordinate number of popular book titles published this century have chosen Garamond, but its usage isn't limited to the literary world. Its extreme popularity has crept into nearly every corner of modern life.

When Apple launched the Macintosh in 1984, it developed a proprietary version of Garamond for its introduction. This Garamond dominated Apple's marketing and became a major part of their brand recognition for nearly two decades.

Nintendo chose italic Garamond in 1985 to describe the versions on their 1985 game consoles. Fifteen years later, Nintendo named a character Garamond—a successful author—in their RPG video game Super Paper Mario.

Though using a common font for a corporate logo can restrict trademark laws and protections, Abercrombie & Fitch chose a Garamond typeface for their famous logo, which is why it looks so familiar to you as it is printed on this page.

The same can be said for Neutrogena, who has proudly imprinted their Garamond logo on their famous bars of soap for decades, as well as their other products and accompanying packaging.

As the Garamond typeset approaches its 400th birthday, it seems there is no sign of slowing for this classic font. It may prove just as popular in another 400 years.

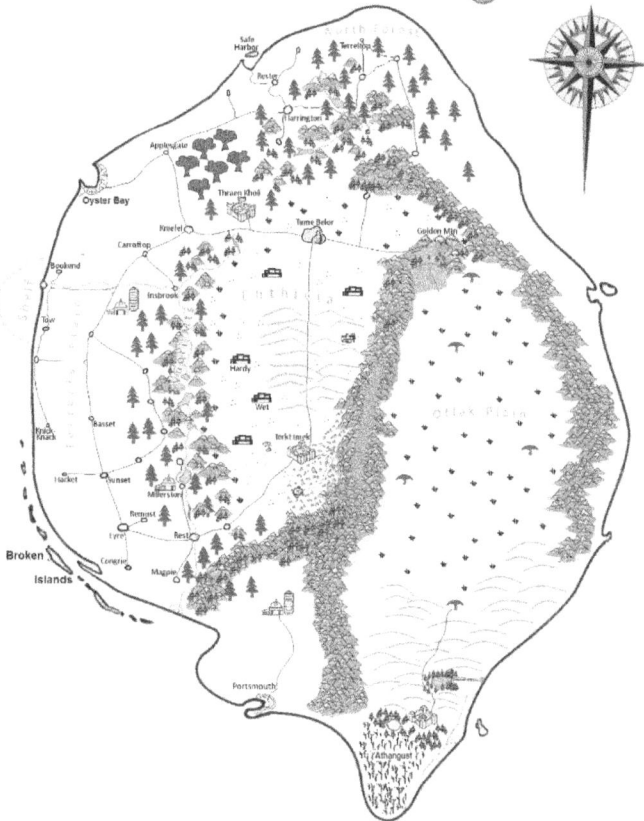